Homeschooling

Other Books of Related Interest:

Opposing Viewpoints Series

Education

At Issue Series

Has No Child Left Behind Been Good for Education?

Current Controversies Series

Homeschooling

"Congress shall make
no law . . . abridging
the freedom of speech,
or of the press."

First Amendment to the U.S. Constitution

The basic foundation of our democracy is the First Amendment guarantee of freedom of expression. The Opposing Viewpoints Series is dedicated to the concept of this basic freedom and the idea that it is more important to practice it than to enshrine it.

**OPPOSING
VIEWPOINTS®
SERIES**

Homeschooling

Noah Berlatsky, book editor

GREENHAVEN PRESS
A part of Gale, Cengage Learning

Detroit • New York • San Francisco • New Haven, Conn • Waterville, Maine • London

GALE
CENGAGE Learning™

Christine Nasso, *Publisher*
Elizabeth Des Chenes, *Managing Editor*

© 2010 Greenhaven Press, a part of Gale, Cengage Learning.

Gale and Greenhaven Press are registered trademarks used herein under license.

For more information, contact:
Greenhaven Press
27500 Drake Rd.
Farmington Hills, MI 48331-3535
Or you can visit our Internet site at gale.cengage.com

For product information and technology assistance, contact us at

Gale Customer Support, 1-800-877-4253
For permission to use material from this text or product, submit all requests online at
www.cengage.com/permissions

Further permissions questions can be emailed to permissionrequest@cengage.com

Articles in Greenhaven Press anthologies are often edited for length to meet page requirements. In addition, original titles of these works are changed to clearly present the main thesis and to explicitly indicate the author's opinion. Every effort is made to ensure that Greenhaven Press accurately reflects the original intent of the authors. Every effort has been made to trace the owners of copyrighted material.

Cover Image copyright Plush Studios/Blend Images/Getty Images and Lauren Nicole/Getty Images.

LIBRARY OF CONGRESS CATALOGING-IN-PUBLICATION DATA

Homeschooling / Noah Berlatsky, book editor.
     p. cm. -- (Opposing viewpoints)
  Includes bibliographical references and index.
  ISBN 978-0-7377-4968-7 (hardcover) -- ISBN 978-0-7377-4969-4 (pbk.)
  1. Home schooling--United States--Juvenile literature. I. Berlatsky, Noah.
  LC40.H6412 2010
  371.04'2--dc22

                                                         2009053379

Printed in the United States of America
1 2 3 4 5 6 7 14 13 12 11 10

Contents

Chapter 3: Who Should Homeschool?

Chapter 4: What Methods Should Homeschoolers Use?

Why Consider Opposing Viewpoints?

> *"The only way in which a human being can make some approach to knowing the whole of a subject is by hearing what can be said about it by persons of every variety of opinion and studying all modes in which it can be looked at by every character of mind. No wise man ever acquired his wisdom in any mode but this."*
>
> John Stuart Mill

In our media-intensive culture it is not difficult to find differing opinions. Thousands of newspapers and magazines and dozens of radio and television talk shows resound with differing points of view. The difficulty lies in deciding which opinion to agree with and which "experts" seem the most credible. The more inundated we become with differing opinions and claims, the more essential it is to hone critical reading and thinking skills to evaluate these ideas. Opposing Viewpoints books address this problem directly by presenting stimulating debates that can be used to enhance and teach these skills. The varied opinions contained in each book examine many different aspects of a single issue. While examining these conveniently edited opposing views, readers can develop critical thinking skills such as the ability to compare and contrast authors' credibility, facts, argumentation styles, use of persuasive techniques, and other stylistic tools. In short, the Opposing Viewpoints Series is an ideal way to attain the higher-level thinking and reading skills so essential in a culture of diverse and contradictory opinions.

In addition to providing a tool for critical thinking, Opposing Viewpoints books challenge readers to question their own strongly held opinions and assumptions. Most people form their opinions on the basis of upbringing, peer pressure, and personal, cultural, or professional bias. By reading carefully balanced opposing views, readers must directly confront new ideas as well as the opinions of those with whom they disagree. This is not to simplistically argue that everyone who reads opposing views will—or should—change his or her opinion. Instead, the series enhances readers' understanding of their own views by encouraging confrontation with opposing ideas. Careful examination of others' views can lead to the readers' understanding of the logical inconsistencies in their own opinions, perspective on why they hold an opinion, and the consideration of the possibility that their opinion requires further evaluation.

Evaluating Other Opinions

To ensure that this type of examination occurs, Opposing Viewpoints books present all types of opinions. Prominent spokespeople on different sides of each issue as well as well-known professionals from many disciplines challenge the reader. An additional goal of the series is to provide a forum for other, less known, or even unpopular viewpoints. The opinion of an ordinary person who has had to make the decision to cut off life support from a terminally ill relative, for example, may be just as valuable and provide just as much insight as a medical ethicist's professional opinion. The editors have two additional purposes in including these less known views. One, the editors encourage readers to respect others' opinions—even when not enhanced by professional credibility. It is only by reading or listening to and objectively evaluating others' ideas that one can determine whether they are worthy of consideration. Two, the inclusion of such viewpoints encourages the important critical thinking skill of objectively evaluating an author's credentials and bias. This evaluation will illuminate an author's reasons for taking a particular stance on an issue and will aid in readers' evaluation of the author's ideas.

It is our hope that these books will give readers a deeper understanding of the issues debated and an appreciation of the complexity of even seemingly simple issues when good and honest people disagree. This awareness is particularly important in a democratic society such as ours in which people enter into public debate to determine the common good. Those with whom one disagrees should not be regarded as enemies but rather as people whose views deserve careful examination and may shed light on one's own.

Thomas Jefferson once said that "difference of opinion leads to inquiry, and inquiry to truth." Jefferson, a broadly educated man, argued that "if a nation expects to be ignorant and free . . . it expects what never was and never will be." As individuals and as a nation, it is imperative that we consider the opinions of others and examine them with skill and discernment. The Opposing Viewpoints Series is intended to help readers achieve this goal.

David L. Bender and Bruno Leone,
Founders

Introduction

> *"Homeschooling is not homogeneous. By design, homeschoolers are opinionated. Our reasons for homeschooling are as varied as our methodologies."*
>
> *—Natalie C. West,*
> *June 28, 2006, on the blog*
> *Ramblings, Rants & Remedies*

In many people's minds, homeschooling is widely associated with the conservative fundamentalist evangelical Christian community. This assumption is not completely off the mark: Committed Christians have long played an important role in homeschooling. According to a January 9, 2009, article by Dan Gilgoff in *U.S. News & World Report,* evangelical Christians accounted for about two-thirds of homeschoolers in 2000.

Unsurprisingly, therefore, the most influential homeschooling advocacy group in the country, the Home School Legal Defense Association (HSLDA), is a Christian organization that often takes conservative views. For example, Michael Farris, cofounder, chairman, and general counsel of HSLDA, wrote a letter to the *Washington Post* in which he stated his opposition to Democratic presidential candidate Barack Obama. According to Farris, an Obama presidency "could be particularly harmful to the American family and the home school community." Farris was particularly concerned that Obama would support the UN Committee on the Rights of the Child, which attempts to set forth universal rights for children. Farris worried that such a statement of human rights would interfere with parental decisions about what is best for children.

While conservative Christians are a large component of the homeschooling movement, they are not by any means the only homeschoolers. Mitchell L. Stevens, in his 2001 book

Kingdom of Children: Culture and Controversy in the Homeschooling Movement, wrote, "At first glance, homeschooling appears to be the logical purview of evangelical and fundamentalist Christians. In fact, one would be hard-pressed to find a social movement peopled by a wider spectrum of faiths and philosophies." Stevens adds that onlookers often find it hard to imagine what "fundamentalists and atheists, Muslims and Mormons, Buddhists and Baptists" could all agree upon. He explains that all share a belief "that children have enormous potential for distinctive accomplishments and that standardized ways of educating children temper or even squelch this potential." Homeschoolers distrust "state intrusion into family life and generally are skeptical of the ability of bureaucracies ... to meet the task of child rearing." Stevens concludes by pointing out that this belief in children and distrust of government is shared by many Americans, and that as a result, homeschooling appeals to a wide range of people.

Messiah College professor Milton Gaither, in a summer 2008 essay in *Educational Horizons,* agreed that while homeschooling had its roots partially in the Christian evangelical movement, it also had important links to secular liberal groups. Gaither argues that in the 1960s and 1970s, countercultural hippie groups on the Left and conservative Christian groups on the Right all reacted against the power of the state. They particularly took a stand against what they saw as the indoctrination and interference of the public school system, which was growing larger, more bureaucratic, and less responsive to the needs of individual parents. Gaither concludes, "Having rejected the mainstream, denizens of both Left and Right looked for personal fulfillment within small, alternative communities. The social and political changes of the second half of the twentieth century made bedfellows of both radical leftists who wanted nothing to do with conventional America and conventional Americans who wanted nothing to do with a country that in their view had sold out to the radical Left."

To some extent, Christian and secular homeschoolers have been able to work together toward common goals. Thus, HSLDA itself says that it is committed to advocating not only for evangelicals, but also for all homeschoolers, whether they are or are not Christian. "Although our officers and directors are Christians, HSLDA membership is not limited to religiously based homeschoolers," the association notes on its Web site.

At the same time, tensions between Christian and non-Christian homeschoolers do exist. Jerry A. Coyne, a biologist at the University of Chicago, discussed one source of controversy in a post on his blog, Why Evolution Is True, on April 27, 2009. Coyne reprinted a letter from a secular homeschooler who writes, "There is a serious problem in homeschooling right now in that most homeschooling families find themselves using the Apologia series for teaching science because it is so parent friendly. However, this series was written with one purpose in mind, and that was to debunk evolution." The writer of the letter goes on to say that no comparable parent-friendly, non-creationist curriculum for secular homeschoolers exists. In this case, the writer suggests that the perception that homeschooling appeals to a mainly Christian audience limits the choices of secular homeschoolers.

If this is the case now, it may well change. The number of homeschoolers is on the rise, growing by 74 percent between 2000 and 2009, according to Dan Gilgoff in the 2009 *U.S. News & World Report* article mentioned earlier. Moreover, the largest area of growth appears to be among non-evangelicals. While evangelicals made up about two-thirds of homeschoolers in 2000, by 2009, Gilgoff reports, they made up slightly more than half. Evangelicals will likely always play a role in the homeschooling movement, but it seems likely that their role in the future will not be as dominant—both within the movement and in public perceptions of it—as it has been in the past. The authors in *Opposing Viewpoints: Homeschooling* look at the changing nature of homeschooling in the following chapters: How Does Homeschooling Affect Children? How Should Homeschooling Be Regulated? Who Should Homeschool? and What Methods Should Homeschoolers Use? The answers to these questions will have a major impact on a future in which homeschoolers and different types of homeschooling become increasingly more prevalent.

How Does Homeschooling Affect Children?

Chapter Preface

One way to discover how homeschooling has affected children is to find men and women who were homeschooled as children and ask them whether and how they think it helped or harmed them.

A large number of former homeschoolers, in fact, have talked publicly about their experiences. Many grown homeschoolers are enthusiastic about their experiences and feel that homeschooling prepared them well for college and life. Carleton Kendrick, writing on FamilyEducation.com, reported that during a panel discussion at the "Growing Without Schooling" conference in Waltham, Massachusetts, in 2009, several former homeschoolers talked about the positive impact homeschooling had had on their lives. Amanda, who works at a legal publishing company while attending the University of Pennsylvania part-time, said that homeschooling helped her learn to balance work and class. In contrast to Amanda, a former homeschooler named Mae had never gone to school and continued to live at home with her parents as an adult. But, Mae said, this was what she wanted to do. She concluded, "Because my parents closed no doors, but continued to support me and to trust my needs, I was able to find a place in the community, yet keep the ties to my family intact at the same time."

Not all former homeschoolers are as positive about their experiences. A writer named Chandra argues in a March 10, 2009, post to her blog, Dispelled: One Girls Journey, that homeschooling is a "cult" in which parents desperately try to isolate their children from contact with the outside world. Chandra says in a March 6 post that her experiences as a homeschooler led her to clinical depression and attempted suicide.

Obviously, different homeschoolers may have different experiences. Beyond anecdotal evidence, however, some studies of grown homeschoolers have been done. These studies indicate that homeschoolers tend to go on to college, obtain college degrees, vote, and participate in community service at higher rates than their non-homeschooled peers. Adult homeschoolers are also twice as likely as non-homeschooled adults to say that they are "very happy" with their lives, according to Frank Vahid in the book *Homeschooling: A Path Rediscovered for Socialization, Education, and Family*. Vahid notes that this data "does not prove that homeschooling better prepares people for the real world, due largely to self-selection . . . present in the homeschool population. However, the . . . data does show that homeschoolers are clearly doing well in the real world." The following viewpoints look at more evidence of how and the ways in which homeschooling has affected children.

> "In 2003, the latest year for which fig-
> ures are available, a record 129 home-
> schoolers were named National Merit
> Scholars, an increase of more than 600
> percent over 1995."

Homeschooling Students Score Comparably to Others on Standardized Tests

Andrea Neal

Andrea Neal is an author and contributor to the Saturday Evening Post, *a bimonthly American magazine. In the following viewpoint, she presents the academic achievements of many homeschoolers. Neal notes that not long ago, homeschoolers were thought of as oddball characters, but now they are academically outperforming many government educated students. She concludes that the structure of homeschooling provides a place for children to thrive.*

Andrea Neal, "Homeschoolers: Into the Mainstream: Excelling in and out of the Home, Homeschooled Kids Are Thriving Across the Country. Students Demonstrating Exceptional Academic Honors Are Capturing the Top Slots at National Competitions," *Saturday Evening Post*, September-October 2006.Copyright © 2006 Saturday Evening Post Society. Reproduced by permission.

As you read, consider the following questions:

1. As stated in the article, how many homeschooled students were named semifinalists in the Presidential Scholars competition?

2. According to Neal, what is the "key ingredient" of many homeschooling families?

3. In what grade does the achievement test score gap between homeschooled children and public or private school students begin to broaden?

It wasn't so long ago that homeschoolers like Johanna Schilling, Jonathan Gainer and Eli Owens were oddballs in the education landscape. Not anymore.

You name the contest—National Spelling Bee, National Geographic Bee, National Merit Scholarship—and chances are good that homeschool kids have participated, performed with distinction, and won. These days, headlines of academic achievement are as likely to feature homeschooled children as their peers from traditional public and private school settings. Perhaps just as noteworthy, nobody's jaw drops when it happens.

This year [2006], four homeschooled students were named semifinalists in the Presidential Scholars competition, which recognizes the nation's most distinguished high school graduates. The honor served notice of two important trends: one, homeschoolers have entered the mainstream of academic achievement; two, they're being recognized for it.

Homeschoolers' Success

At 17, Johanna was recognized as the first homeschool winner of a $40,000 Ruth DeYoung Kohler Scholarship for artistic merit in her home state of Wisconsin. She will use the money to pursue her studies at the Houghton College school of music in New York.

Eli, 19, a homeschool graduate who attends West Virginia University, was named a 2006–2007 Goldwater Scholar in March. He was one of 323 college students nationally to receive the award, established by Congress to encourage advanced studies by select sophomores and juniors who excel in math, science and engineering.

Jonathan, 14, was the first homeschooler picked for the Kelley Junior Executive Institute, a summer program at Indiana University that identifies 50 high-achieving, primarily minority high school students interested in studying business. Note that he's the age of a typical eighth grader, yet he's already completed Algebra II.

These stories are just the tip of the iceberg. In 2005, a homeschooler won the National Geographic Bee. Homeschoolers swept the first three spots in the 2000 National Spelling Bee. In 2003, the latest year for which figures are available, a record 129 homeschoolers were named National Merit Scholars, an increase of more than 600 percent over 1995. The estimated 1.8 million homeschoolers—out of 54 million children in kindergarten through high school—seem to be achieving honors disproportionate to their numbers.

"It's not surprising that a homeschooler gets much better academic results. There's just no way around the structure," says Ian Slatter, director of media relations for the Home School Legal Defense Association in Virginia.

Structure Matters

Yes, structure matters. Although it varies by family, the typical homeschool consists of one parent teaching one or more children in the home. But not just in the home. Homeschoolers take field trips and visit museums and libraries. They network with other homeschool families. They use books and curricula that reflect their own academic and religious values, yet align closely enough to state academic standards that students are prepared for standardized tests, which some states require. In

SAT Test Scores by School Type

2001 data

	Home School	Public School	Private–Independent School	Private–Religious School
SAT total				
Test score raw	1,093.1	1,012.6	1,123.8	1,055.6
Predicted score	1,054.5	1,021.1	1,064.4	1,050.5
SAT Math				
Test score raw	526.5	510.1	566.9	523.3
Predicted score	527.7	513.1	534.8	528.0
SAT Verbal				
Test score raw	566.6	502.6	556.9	532.3
Predicted score	526.7	507.8	529.6	522.6

TAKEN FROM: Clive R. Belfield, "Home-schoolers: How Well Do They Perform on the SAT for College Admissions?" in Bruce S. Cooper, ed. *Home Schooling in Fullview: A Reader.* Greenwich, CT: Information Age Publishing, 2005, p. 172.

a homeschool, the teacher-student ratio for any given lesson is 1:1 or 1:2. Not even an elite private school, where class size is capped at 16 or 18, can rival that.

The structure works especially well in the elementary years as students are mastering math and reading skills that will be the foundation for later learning. When course work grows more complex, many homeschool families contract with experts to teach their children more advanced subjects, sometimes pooling resources to create small classrooms not too different from a traditional school.

It's the flexibility that so many homeschooling families lift up as the key ingredient. In a homeschool, parents can quickly identify a student's areas of strength and weakness, offering enrichment opportunities for the former and focused attention on the latter.

Those with a gift for music can take instrument lessons or catch a symphony matinee when their traditional classmates are in school. Johanna, for example, spent up to three hours a day practicing piano for 10 years. Computer whizzes can seek out apprenticeships with nearby businesses; those who love sports can finish their workout in the morning before the YMCA gets crowded.

Because of structure and flexibility, the typical homeschool student can complete graduation requirements by age 16. As a result, some go to college early; many enroll in local community colleges until their parents deem them ready to live on a campus with older students.

But it's not always been an easy road for families wishing to homeschool. Until recently, state laws and regulations deterred all but the most committed parents from opting out of the regular school system.

Historians trace the modern homeschool movement to the 1960s, when social reformers and counterculture activists questioned the benefits of the conventional school day, with its regimen of discipline and structured learning. That movement was short-lived, in part because it saw itself as a form of civil disobedience, unconcerned with changing laws to facilitate the legal homeschooling of children.

After the Supreme Court struck down school prayer as unconstitutional in 1963, a conservative and explicitly Christian movement arose to pull children out of what was seen as an increasingly secular and valueless school system.

The Start of Homeschooling

Throughout the 1970s, Slatter notes, homeschooling was essentially illegal in 45 states, where teacher-certification laws permitted only licensed teachers to instruct students of compulsory school age, typically six to 16. Slatter's group was formed in 1983 to lobby to change those laws and practices that impeded homeschooling and to help families navigate regulations. By 1993, all 50 states had recognized a parent's right to homeschool.

Around the same time, a homeschooling industry arose offering training programs and curricular materials for families getting started. *Home Education Magazine*, based in Washington State, has been published for more than 20 years and features articles and columns about effective practices. Today, homeschool support groups and Internet-based clearinghouses can be found at the click of a mouse.

Although evangelical Christians remain the single biggest group in the homeschooling movement, they are by no means the only ones. In her book *Homeschoolers' Success Stories*, Linda Dobson notes that "families from every conceivable religious, economic, political, and philosophical background in the United States" have realized the benefits to homeschooling.

"This wave has been impelled by homeschooling's greater visibility as an educational option; local, state, and national homeschooling support groups; easy networking and information sharing via the Internet and e-mail; and continuing government-school problems, such as dumbed-down curriculum, violence, drugs, bullying, and more," she writes.

Slatter, whose group is Christian-based but will assist all home schoolers regardless of faith, says the reasons for opting out of public schools haven't changed much in 20 years. "Consistently, the two top reasons for homeschooling include the negative peer environment of public schools. We're talking about drugs, crime and negative peer influences. There's also the lack of a biblical worldview or any sort of religious teaching. No education is values-free. A public school that is actually going to be teaching will inevitably undermine the religious values parents will be teaching."

Understanding and Accepting Homeschool Programs

What has changed is public understanding and acceptance of the homeschool phenomenon. The percentage of those feeling that homeschooling is a "bad thing" dropped from 73 percent in 1985 to 57 percent in 1997, according to a Phi Delta Kappa (PDK)/Gallup poll. In a 1999 poll, PDK asked if public schools should make services available to children who are schooled at home, and a surprising number of respondents said yes. The numbers ranged from a high of 92 percent for special education courses for disabled or handicapped children to a low of 53 percent for transportation services.

There are critics, to be sure, including members of the National Education Association, the powerful teachers' union. "Don't most parents have a tough enough job teaching their children social, disciplinary and behavioral skills?" asks one such skeptic in an opinion column posted on the NEA Web site. Dave Arnold, a member of the Illinois Education Association, suggests it's better to leave formal education to professionals. Parents, he said, "would be wise to help their children and themselves by leaving the responsibility of teaching math, science, art, writing, history, geography and other subjects to those who are knowledgeable, trained and motivated to do the best job possible."

The data, however, are on the homeschoolers' side.

In the most significant study to date, "Scholastic Achievement and Demographic Characteristics of Home School Students in 1998," researcher Lawrence M. Rudner made the following findings:

- Almost 25 percent of homeschool students are enrolled one or more grades above their age-level peers in public and private schools.

- Homeschool student achievement test scores are exceptionally high. The median scores for every subtest at every grade (typically in the 70th to 80th percentile) are well above those of public and Catholic/private school students.

- On average, homeschool students in grades one to four perform one grade level above their age-level public or private school peers on achievement tests.

- The achievement test score gap between homeschool students and public or private school students starts to widen in grade five.

- Students who have been homeschooled their entire academic lives have higher scholastic achievement test scores than students who have also attended other educational programs.

Smaller studies have affirmed the findings, and Slatter says his organization hopes to do an updated achievement study in the near future.

The Proof Is in the Children

Homeschool families are gratified by the research but say the real proof can be seen in their well-adjusted and well-rounded children. Ariana and Jonathan Gainer of Indianapolis are a case in point. Both spent two years in a private school, which they liked; both endorse the flexibility that homeschooling gives them to pursue their passions.

Ariana, 12, loves to read and write. She is active in her church and involved with Y-Press, a news-reporting network that allows young people to experience journalism firsthand and get their work published in the *Indianapolis Star*. At the moment, Ariana is researching a story on rumspringa, the time when Amish children are released from their church's control to decide if they will accept the faith of their families.

Jonathan envisions a career as a CEO, a dream bolstered by his time at the Kelley School of Business Summer Institute at Indiana University. While there, Jonathan headed up a team of five students responsible for developing a business plan from conception through presentation to stockholders. The team's idea—a cell phone company with global, wireless Internet subscriptions—was researched so well that it won first place in the institute competition. The experience was invaluable, Jonathan says, because he got to work with other students on a team and learn in a more collaborative way than he is accustomed.

Their parents, Marvin and Jerrilyn Gainer, first got a taste of homeschooling when they served as missionaries in Mexico and the children were just preschool age. For Marvin, a stint as a substitute teacher in the Indianapolis public school system solidified his belief that homeschooling would be right for their children.

The Columbine High School shooting rampage had just occurred, and Marvin says he fully understood how it could happen. He recalls "total chaos in the hallways . . . total disrespect students had toward teachers" and the inability of principals to impose adequate discipline to get things under control.

"There was nothing going on there that impressed me. For a kid to do well in that system, they had to spend so much energy trying to survive. I just didn't want that for my kids."

Now, with their own children thriving, the Gainers have launched an educational center in inner-city Indianapolis where homeschooling families can come together for specialized instruction. They seek out the top people in their fields to teach upper-level and Advanced Placement courses, such as etymology, biology and calculus. Families share the costs.

The center creates opportunities for socialization but, better yet, makes available the kind of teaching typically associated with elite private schools. Yes, homeschools have entered the mainstream of America's educational system, and their students intend to compete with the best and brightest in the country.

| "How can the education of a student in-
structed in creationism possibly be considered equivalent to that of one taught
legitimate science?"

Homeschooling Curricula Do Not Meet Academic Standards

Steve Shives

*Steve Shives is an online writer and critic. In the following view-
point, he argues that many homeschool parents are religious
conservatives who teach their children creationism rather than
evolution. Shives argues that parents should have the right to
teach their children what they wish. He maintains, however, that
creationism is not science. Therefore, he says, homeschool or
other students who learn creationism instead of evolution should
not receive a high school diploma from the state.*

As you read, consider the following questions:

1. According to Shives, what is the area of study most affected by the Christian bent of homeschooling?

2. According to Shives, how many papers demonstrating the credibility of creationism have appeared in peer-reviewed scientific journals?

3. What kind of instructors, in Shives's opinion, should ideally teach children?

There are many, many things I find dubious about the practice of parents homeschooling their children. I wonder how a mother or father who has not been educated as a teacher, who in many cases has not even been to college her/himself, can possibly provide [her/his] child with as good an education as students receive in our much-maligned public schools. And I can't help but think that these homeschool students, of whom there are several million in the United States, are being robbed of a crucial formative experience by not attending school with other people their age and being forced to interact with a diverse group of peers.

Fundamentalism and Education

Most disturbing is the virulent strain of religious fundamentalism that is found in the lessons being taught [to] homeschooled children, especially in the United States. Not all American homeschooling is religious—that's not what I'm saying. I've known people personally who were homeschooled from a secular curriculum, and there are many others like them throughout the country. I think I'm safe in saying, however, that the majority of homeschooling in the U.S. is religious—specifically, fundamentalist Christian—in nature. This is no big secret.

(UPDATE: Thanks to a little belated research on my part, and the comments of a few homeschooling parents, I must now say that the percentage of fundamentalist Christians in homeschool in the U.S. is not as overwhelming as I state above. The National Center for Education Statistics conducted a study in 2003 in which 72% of participating homeschool parents surveyed cited "To provide religious or moral instruction" as a reason for homeschooling their children, with 30% citing that as their most important reason. So apparently the big secret is that the majority of homeschool families probably *aren't* fundamentalist Christians, and they resent the assumption, thank you very much. I stand corrected.)

The area of study most affected by the Christian bent of homeschooling is science. The religion of the guy who wrote the textbook might not matter a whole lot when you're studying geometry or reading *Romeo and Juliet*, but it comes into play in a big way when you hit high school–level biology. Homeschool parents who get their biology curriculum from sources like Apologia [a company that provides a homeschool creationist science curriculum] are not teaching their children science. They are giving them a Sunday school lesson.

Creationism Is Not Science

Instead of evolutionary biology, which has been the keystone of the life sciences for over 150 years, homeschool students are taught creationism—that the God of the Bible personally created the universe more or less as described in the book of Genesis. There are several varieties of creationism—Young Earth, Old Earth, Omphalosian, Neo—all thoroughly discredited. Increasingly, it is dressed in the pseudoscientific trappings of intelligent design [the argument that living things must have been created by an intelligent designer]. Whatever its proponents choose to call it, regardless of the intellectual contortions it performs to make the biblical creation account plausible, it isn't science and it should never be taught as such.

But it is taught as science to millions of children and teenagers all over the country. Worse yet, many overtly religious homeschool organizations are empowered by their state governments to grant high school diplomas to students who have completed the required courses, with more attention paid to the title of a given course rather than the content. How can the education of a student instructed in creationism possibly be considered equivalent to that of one taught legitimate science?

One such diploma-granting homeschool organization is the Mason Dixon Homeschoolers Association (MDHSA), headquartered in Waynesboro, Pennsylvania, not far from where I live. The MDHSA is an overtly fundamentalist Christian organization that uses the creationist Apologia Biology curriculum in its science courses. Its Web site contains a "Statement of Purpose" and excerpts from its bylaws, with which all members must agree if they wish to have full voting and office-holding privileges within the group. Among the bylaws excerpted on the Web site:

> The Bible is the inspired and infallible Word of God and constitutes completed and final revelation. The Bible, in its original autograph, is without error in whole and in part, including theological concepts as well as geographical and historical details. . . .

"Biblical literalists" would be putting, it mildly.

Unacceptable Materials

Also on the Web site, as a downloadable.pdf file, is a list of course descriptions for MDHSA's Assisted Learning Program Service [ALPS], which provides lesson plans for high school–level homeschool students. The description for the biology course, with Apologia Biology as its source text, naturally, reads in part:

> The course will include an introduction to the philosophy and history of biological science, introductory biochemistry, and a review of evolutionary theory and creation theory.

Other materials offered by Apologia include the book *Unlocking the Mysteries of Creation: The Explorer's Guide to the*

Awesome Works of God and the DVD *Icons of Evolution*, described as "a hard-hitting examination of the major errors and omissions in evolutionary theory that are presented as 'facts' in today's high school and college textbooks." Something tells me the biology class's review of evolutionary theory won't be worth much.

There is also an ALPS course entitled Physical Science, again using an Apologia textbook, whose course description promises to "especially concentrate on the myths generated by the hysterical environmentalist movement." Clearly, there are axes to grind here; clearly, the education of the students is not a paramount concern.

The description of the Physical Science course also claims, "It is an excellent course for preparing the student to take a college prep high school science curriculum." I can tell you as a firsthand eyewitness that this is total crap. When I took a basic college-level general biology course last year [2007], one of my classmates was a girl who had attended a Christian private school. Instead of legitimate science, she had been taught creationism, and thus didn't know the first thing about what actual biological theory tells us regarding the origins of the universe and the development of life on Earth. She was not a stupid person, but her religious fundamentalist teachers had prevented her from learning some of the most rudimentary scientific knowledge. She may have been prepared to continue her academic career at Liberty University [an Evangelical Baptist university in Lynchburg, VA, which teaches creationism], but a first-year community college course in real science was utterly beyond her grasp.

Do Not Accredit Creationism

Parents who homeschool their children in this way might respond by invoking their constitutionally guaranteed religious liberties. I'm not suggesting their right to worship be infringed upon in the slightest. Freedom of religion is an el-

Homeschooling Is Opposed to Science

I'm troubled by the fact that a significant percentage of home-schooling parents choose this option because of an overriding feeling that they want their children to pursue curricula from theology . . . rather than a scientific perspective.

I wonder how many of these types of home-schooled kids take the . . . lack of respect for scientific inquiry into adulthood.

Russell Shaw, "Let's Restrict Home Schooling,"
Huffington Post, *May 21, 2007. www.huffingtonpost.com.*

ementary human right, as much as freedom of speech or the right to due process of law, and it must always be protected. I'm not nuts about homeschooling, be it religious or secular, but as long as it's legal, I say parents should be allowed to teach their children whatever they see fit to teach them.

But here's the catch—and I'm afraid I must insist: If a homeschool organization, such as the MDHSA, wants to be recognized by its state government as an accredited diploma-granting institution, it must teach legitimate science, including evolutionary biology.

The religious beliefs of Christian parents are irrelevant to the issue. Creationism is not science, and neither is its gussied-up twin intelligent design. There is no serious scientific debate on this question. There has never been a single paper published in a peer-reviewed scientific journal demonstrating that creationism/intelligent design has the tiniest shred of credibility. It is the very definition of an exploded hypothesis. Biblical literalists are free to believe that the world came into being exactly as Genesis tells it, but their belief does not refute the impartially observed, irrefutable facts.

To give this a bit more proportion, imagine that you have a student attending public school and you learn that he or she is being taught in history class that American Indians are the descendants of a lost tribe of Israelites migrating to the continent thousands of years ago, or that the Holocaust is a Zionist myth, or in math class that the precise value of π is 3. Would your judgment be that your child was receiving a suitable historical or mathematical education? I think most reasonable parents would say no. The same standards should apply to science as to history and math.

The education of children is essential to the survival and positive progress of human society. Children should be taught (ideally by qualified, credentialed instructors) to read and write, to understand the basic principles of mathematics, and to understand and appreciate the beauty and complexity of the natural world through science. If you also want to teach your child about salvation through Jesus Christ, or the flood of Noah, go for it. You have, and should always have, that freedom. It's the birthright of every human being.

A high school diploma, on the other hand, isn't a birthright. It's something that must be earned. The states have the right and the responsibility to award those diplomas only to students who have adequately completed their education. That group should not include anyone whose science studies omit evolutionary biology and include a credulous literal reading of the Bible. Those students—be they homeschoolers or attendees of religious private schools—have been cheated, and before they get to graduate, their misguided teachers should have to make good.

> "[Thomas Smedley's] results showed
> that homeschooled children had greater
> social skills and maturity than students
> attending public school. The differences
> were rather dramatic."

Homeschooling Students Are Well Socialized

Minnesota Homeschoolers' Alliance

The Minnesota Homeschoolers' Alliance (MHA) is a nonsectarian, nonprofit organization, which provides information and support to homeschooling families in Minnesota. In the following viewpoint, MHA argues that academic studies have shown homeschoolers to be better socialized than their public school peers. MHA also says that talking to and interacting with homeschoolers shows that they are well socialized. Indeed, MHA maintains, one would expect homeschoolers to be well socialized, since they interact with people of all ages, rather than just with children their own ages.

As you read, consider the following questions:

1. What age were the children studied by Dr. Larry Shyers?

Minnesota Homeschoolers' Alliance, "What About Socialization?" October 13, 2005. www.homeschoolers.org. Copyright © MHA. Reproduced by permission.

2. According to MHA, what is the best thing to do if one is concerned about a homeschooler's socialization?

3. According to MHA, why do seasoned homeschoolers laugh when others suggest that their children are "avoiding the real world"?

If you're thinking about homeschooling, you've probably wondered how your children will be socialized. If you're already a homeschooler, you've been asked about this many, many times. Each family will answer the question differently, but here's some food for thought as you form your own views on socialization.

What Is Socialization?

First, what is meant by socialization? The next time you're asked the "S" question, ask the person how *they* define socialization. You may be surprised by their answer. For some people, socialization means "not being different." For others it means "being able to get along with others." Still others would say it means "learning to do that stuff we did in school—you know, waiting in lines, raising our hands—those types of things." It will be hard to provide an answer to the socialization question until you know what's really being asked.

Dictionary definitions of socialization vary somewhat by publisher, but generally speaking, "socialization" is defined as "the process of learning to interact appropriately with other members of society." We'll use that definition here as we look at the socialization of homeschooled children from three perspectives: academic research, anecdotal evidence, and common sense.

Academic Research

The socialization of homeschooled children has been studied many times, but summaries of the academic literature almost invariably refer to the 1992 studies of Thomas Smedley, M.S., and Dr. Larry Shyers.

Mr. Smedley's master's thesis at Radford University in Virginia was titled "The Socialization of Homeschool Children." He used the Vineland Adaptive Behavior Scales to assess the personal and social skills of matched groups of homeschooled and publicly schooled students. His results showed that homeschooled children had greater social skills and maturity than students attending public school. The differences were rather dramatic, with the homeschooled students ranking in the 84th percentile, while the public school students scored only in the 27th percentile. Smedley noted that public school students are socialized "horizontally" into conformity by their same-age peers, while homeschooled students are socialized "vertically" toward responsibility and adulthood by their parents.

Dr. Shyers's study went a step further. For his doctoral dissertation, "Comparison of Social Adjustment Between Home and Traditionally Schooled Students," he compared the actual *behaviors* of two groups of seventy children from the ages of eight to ten. One group was homeschooled and the other group was drawn from public and private schools. This was a "blind" study, in which the children's behaviors were evaluated by trained observers who did not know which of the students were homeschooled and which were not. The . . . Direct Observation Form [of the Child Behavior Checklist] was used to categorize each child's conduct while playing in mixed groups of children from both sample groups. The homeschooled children were found to have significantly fewer problem behaviors than the children from public and private schools.

Additional studies regularly appear in the academic literature. They support and supplement the work of Smedley and Shyers, painting an overwhelmingly positive picture of the socialization of homeschooled students. It's very clear that homeschoolers learn to "interact appropriately with other members of society" while learning at home.

> # Parents Should Socialize Children
>
> Dr. Raymond Moore ... has done extensive research on homeschooling and socialization. . . . "The idea that children need to be around many other youngsters in order to be 'socialized,'" Dr. Moore writes, "is perhaps the most dangerous . . . myth in education and child rearing today."
>
> Children often do not respond well to large groups. . . . After analyzing over 8,000 early childhood studies, Dr. Moore concluded that, contrary to popular belief, children are best socialized by parents—not other children.
>
> *Isabel Shaw, "Social Skills and Homeschooling: Myths and Facts," FamilyEducation.com. http://school.familyeducation.com.*

Anecdotal Evidence

Veteran homeschooling parents have seen hundreds of home-schooled kids and have long since compiled their own anecdotal evidence of socialization. They note that homeschoolers generally "make the news" in positive ways; that homeschoolers tend to be polite, friendly people who get along well with others; and that homeschoolers seem to have a zest for life and learning that institutionally schooled kids sometimes lack.

The myth of homeschoolers being "homebound" has been exploded. Homeschooling's rapid growth has led to a wide variety of social events, particularly in metropolitan areas. Rather than looking for more "socializing" opportunities, many of today's homeschooling families are now trying to determine the best way to *limit* their outside activities.

If you're still wrestling with the socialization issue, one of the best things you can do is compile your own anecdotal evidence. Talk with homeschoolers. Take advantage of any opportunity you have to get to know them. See how they relate to each other and people outside their families. Attend MHA's [Minnesota Homeschoolers' Alliance's] Annual Conference. There you'll see hundreds of homeschooling parents and children interacting with each other. In all likelihood, you'll be amazed at how pleasant and "normal" they are. You may even conclude they're well socialized!

Common Sense

Finally, test the socialization idea with plain old common sense. If the goal of socialization is to learn to interact appropriately with other members of society—people of all ages— would you really expect 30 kids of the same age in a room with one adult to become socially adept? Is it realistic to expect children to learn appropriate "adult world" conduct from their same-age peers?

Seasoned homeschoolers often laugh when a critic suggests that their children won't be properly socialized because they're "avoiding the real world." Homeschooled children *live* in the real world! They have consistent contact with adults leading active lives and with children of all ages, while their schooled peers spend most of their day indoors with other children almost exactly their same age. From a commonsense perspective, would you expect to find academic research and anecdotal evidence of socialization problems in homeschoolers, or in children who have been artificially age-segregated and isolated from life's broader social fabric?

| "*Parents often believe that they are pro-*
tecting their children from the 'evils' of
life. However, children cannot be
brought up in a bell jar."

Homeschooling Students Are Isolated and Poorly Socialized

Margaret W. Boyce

Margaret Boyce is a resident of Saugatuck, Michigan; several of her letters have been published in the Holland Sentinel, *a Michigan newspaper. In the following viewpoint, Boyce argues that the public school system is vital for democracy. Furthermore, she maintains that students who are homeschooled are lonely and ill-equipped to deal with different kinds of people and perspectives. She suggests that parents should volunteer at public schools rather than selfishly try to control all aspects of their childrens' lives.*

As you read, consider the following questions:

1. According to Boyce, what right are homeschooled children being denied?

2. According to the author, what does education include besides a curriculum?

3. What did a recent Harvard study find about the comparative performance of homeschoolers and public school students in college, according to Boyce?

I read with interest the recent article in the [*Holland*] *Sentinel* [the Michigan newspaper in which Boyce's comments appeared] about home-school families. I find it strange that we send our young men and women to help assure that children can go to school in Afghanistan, yet we allow parents in Michigan to keep their children at home.

One of the best and brightest moves that our Founding Fathers made was to make it possible for all children in America, not just the rich, to be educated. Eventually, all children were expected to attend. If they did not, they were considered "truant" and parents were held responsible and could go to jail. This public education still is the very cornerstone of democracy.

This strange phenomenon called "home-schooling" at best undermines these principles. For many children, it is far worse. Who is monitoring these families? Many a child of abusive parents has an observant teacher to thank for a rescue, some for their very lives. To whom can these children turn when they are kept at home? They are being denied a basic right, which has been fought for all the way to the Supreme Court— the right to attend school.

We don't allow people to play doctor or nurse without a license, nor can one play lawyer without passing some rather rigorous tests. But today, anyone who wants to "play school" can do so, regardless of their educational background. Recently, some parents have been jailed for withholding medical treatment for their children, yet we are almost making heroes of these parents who do the same with their children's education.

State Schooling Promotes Democracy

Protecting and promoting the prospective freedom of children by providing them an education that exposes them to and engages them intellectually with the diversity of a pluralist democracy can be threatening to parents. The social critic bell hooks has written of her own childhood, for example, "School was the place of ecstasy—pleasure and danger. To be changed by ideas was pure pleasure. But to learn ideas that ran counter to values and beliefs at home was to place oneself at risk, to enter the danger zone. . . ." But these are risks that must be accepted, for children have an interest in being free persons and parents cannot be entitled to ensure that their child grows up to be exactly the kind of person they want her to be.

Thus, the freedom argument leads to the conclusion that the education of children ought to be regulated in such a way as to guarantee that they learn about and engage with the diversity of ways of life in a democracy. Receiving such an education is one very important way the state can attempt to protect and promote the future freedom and autonomy of children. It is also important, I would add, for civic reasons. . . . The reason is that citizenship in a culturally and religiously diverse liberal democracy requires that each citizen be prepared to recognize that the values that guide his or her life will not be shared by all other citizens. Therefore, each citizen needs to learn to be able to participate democratically with citizens of diverse convictions.

Rob Reich, "Why Home Schooling Should Be Regulated,"
Home Schooling in Full View: A Reader, *ed. Bruce S. Cooper.*
Greenwich, CT: Information Age Publishing, 2005.

Home-Schoolers Miss Stimulation

Some parents of home-schooled children speak glowingly of the "wonderful imaginations" developed by their lonely child, who, being surrounded always by adults, has little opportunities to develop friendships with real children. Others associate only with small groups of like-minded people. What happens when they enter the world and cannot control everything, as they do in their sheltered home environment?

What an ego trip for a parent—to be all things to your children, to control every thought, every concept that enters their world. Is this education, or programming? To deny them the stimulation of working and playing with their peers is unfair. It's far better to send them out into the world for brief forays, such as the school day, and then discuss the day's adventure while they are still young enough to want to work out values with their parents.

There are other losses, such as never being "on the team," never cheering for "our school," never being in a class where the interaction of ideas is more important than the text, or doing any of the myriad of things that make up the process of "belonging," from the first day of school to the 50th class reunion. There is far more to an education than a curriculum—it includes summer break, Friday nights and graduation.

I have met and talked with a variety of home-schoolers, both children and parents. Many have great gaps in their knowledge. Many are incredibly naïve. Some do quite well—they would have been superstars in school. Others can't wait to leave home, knowing full well that they have been cheated.

Homes-Schooling Parents Are Selfish

Parents often believe that they are protecting their children from the "evils" of life. However, children cannot be brought up in a bell jar. Remember that the school day is only six hours long, five days a week. That leaves many hours during the week and summer for the parent.

Give your child the wings needed to grow outside of that jar. If parents wish to be involved in the education of their children, there are many opportunities to be part of the school day. Volunteer to be a lunch or recess monitor. Offer to tutor children in reading or math. Help the art teacher. Be a part of the process of building your community, not a member of the opposition.

A recent Harvard [University] study following home-schooled children over many years found that these children did not do better at the college level than traditionally educated children. The real trip was for the mothers, who received the big emotional rewards. My response is: Mothers, get a life. How unfair is it for you to take away your own child's life in order to gratify yours? Is this what we must expect from the "me first" generation as it raises their families?

The role of a parent is vital in a child's education. However, without all four of the pillars provided by home, school, church and community working together, we have a precarious foundation for the next generation. The public school system is the very cornerstone of democracy in America. We need to cherish it and nurture it.

> "Many Christians who homeschool be-
> lieve that the greatest socialization their
> children can have is to be trained to
> emulate Jesus, who is a servant of
> man."

Homeschooling Provides Christian Socialization

Michael F. Haverluck

*Michael F. Haverluck is a writer and reporter for the Christian
Broadcasting Network (CBN). In the following viewpoint, he argues that studies show that homeschoolers are not poorly socialized compared to their peers. Moreover, he says, the kind of socialization that occurs in public schools is opposed to Christian
ideals of humility, and students who go to public schools often
end up renouncing their Christian faith. For believers, Haverluck
argues, the most important socialization is to grow up with faith
in Jesus, and that kind of socialization is best achieved through
homeschooling.*

Michael F. Haverluck, "Socialization: Homeschooling vs. Schools," *CBN News Online*,
May 2, 2007. www.cbn.com. Copyright © 2007 The Christian Broadcasting Network.
Reproduced by permission

As you read, consider the following questions:

1. According to Haverluck, why are educators and school boards concerned about the exodus of homeschoolers from the public schools?

2. According to Dr. Michael Mitchell, what traits are promoted in conventional schools?

3. According to Caryl Matrisciana, what percentage of public-schooled Americans brought up in Christian households disown their Christian faith by the first year of college?

M any homeschoolers share this sentiment when it comes to public schools, believing that the moral relativism, violence, peer pressure, drugs and promiscuity found inside their gates provide an inadequate setting to properly socialize their children.

Yet 92 percent of superintendents believe that home learners are emotionally unstable, deprived of proper social development and too judgmental of the world around them, according to a California study by researcher Dr. Brian [D.] Ray.

What makes homeschool socialization such a hot topic?

With approximately 4 million children currently being homeschooled in the U.S., along with a 15- to 20-percent yearly growth rate, many professional educators and school boards are concerned that this exodus will keep funds from entering the public education system.

Many teachers also believe that successful home instruction by uncredentialed parents undermines their expertise and jeopardizes their jobs.

Questions about inadequate socialization are often brought up as a means to disqualify homeschooling as a viable alternative form of education, but are the arguments valid?

A look at the research on this socialization debate shines further light on the issue.

Parents Should Be the Primary Influence

Why is there such a dichotomy in the socialization experienced between homeschoolers and conventional students? It all has to do with the learning environment.

The National Home Education Research Institute [NHERI] disclosed that the 36 to 54 hours that students spend in school-related weekly activities make peers and adults outside of the home the primary influences in children's lives—not the parents.

Realizing the harm that this constant exposure can produce, especially if it's not countered by involved parenting, most homeschoolers are well aware of their children's need for close one-to-one contact throughout the education process.

Jesus understood the importance of continual intimate contact with His students, as He ate, slept and fellowshipped with His disciples 24 hours a day. It is unlikely that Jesus would have entrusted their training to strangers.

So how do these different settings affect children? [Researcher] Thomas Smedley believes that homeschoolers have superior socialization skills, and his research supports this claim. He conducted a study in which he administered the Vineland Adaptive Behavior Scales test to identify mature and well-adapted behaviors in children. Home learners ranked in the 84th percentile, compared to publicly schooled students, who were drastically lower in the 27th.

Many school socialization advocates argue that homeschooling precludes children from experiencing real life.

Instead of being locked behind school gates in what some would consider an artificial setting characterized by bells, forced silence and age segregation, homeschoolers frequently extend their everyday classroom to fire departments, hospitals, museums, repair shops, city halls, national parks, churches and colleges, where real community interaction and contacts are made.

Dismantling the stereotype that home learners spend their days isolated from society at kitchen tables with workbooks in hand, NHERI reports that they actually participate in approximately five different social activities outside the home on a regular basis.

Furthermore, researcher Dr. Linda Montgomery found that 78 percent of high school home learners were employed with paying jobs, while a majority engaged in volunteering and community service.

Research presented at the National Christian Home Educators Leadership Conference divulged that homeschool graduates far exceeded their public and private school counterparts in college by ranking the highest in 42 of 63 indicators of collegiate success. They were also ranked as being superior in four out of five achievement categories, including socialization, as they were assessed as being the most charismatic and influential.

Socialization Should Include Jesus

When most home educators and school administrators speak of successful socialization, are they referring to the same thing?

Education researcher Dr. Michael Mitchell found that being popular, aggressively competitive, materialistically driven and self-confident are traits promoted in conventional schools.

His study shows that these campus ideals are discouraged by Christian home educators in favor of building their children's character and dismantling selfish ambitions. Integrity, responsibility, respect for others, trust in God, biblical soundness and an amiable disposition topped the ideal social qualities they desired their youth to embody.

Many Christians who homeschool believe that the greatest socialization their children can have is to be trained to emulate Jesus, who is a servant of man. Home educators examined by Mitchell strive to dismantle any selfish ambitions and self-aggrandizement seen in their children, as opposed to cultivating them.

Getting ahead of one's peers is not consistent with Jesus's urging in Matthew 20:25b–28, which calls for Christians to seek a lowly and servile role to those around them. However, this does not mean that Christians are called to underachieve, as Colossians 3:23 exhorts readers to push for peak performance in every endeavor, but for the glory of God rather than for selfish ambition.

Pride is also promoted in the public schools. It is often repackaged as self-esteem in programs such as "Here's Looking at You, 2000," in which education researcher Dr. Amy Binder reports that students are instructed to believe that they are "the most important person in the world."

Many Christian home educators assert that the kind of pride being taught in the schools is discouraged throughout Scripture by Jesus and Paul, who preach against lifting oneself up or putting oneself first in favor of assuming a lowly position among others, as seen in Luke 14:10–11 and Romans 12:3.

They often contend that traditional students are driven to achieve high marks in order to attain lucrative and prestigious jobs that can lead to lives of self-indulgence, while the Bible calls man not to be overcome by material concerns.

Even though God enjoys prospering His children, He also warns us in 1 Timothy 6:10 that "the love of money is a root of all kinds of evil. Some people, eager for money, have wandered from the faith and pierced themselves with many griefs."

The mass socialization conducted within schools has brought about a proliferation of delinquent behavior within this nation's youth, reports education researcher, Dr. Michael Slavinski. He notes that student bodies are increasingly riddled with violence, drugs, promiscuity, emotional disorders, crime, contempt for authority, desperate behavior, illiteracy and peer dependency—just to name a few.

Today, parents are not as surprised to see reports of fifth-graders having sex in class; hear about school shootings; find drugs or condoms in backpacks; receive phone calls from the police and principals; or witness defiant, apathetic and unrecognizable tones in their children's voices.

"Live and let learn," say many parents. Most home educators are fine with this, as long as their children's learning comes from mature, seasoned and embracing adults who have the children's best interests at heart—above political or economic agendas. They believe that such training shouldn't come from peers either, which amounts to the blind leading the blind.

When the Direct Observation Form of the Child Behavior Checklist was administered by education researcher Dr. Larry Shyers to identify 97 problematic behaviors in two groups of children, traditionally schooled students exuded eight times as many antisocial traits than their homeschooled counterparts. This lies in direct contrast to claims by public school advocates that exposure to campus life leads to proper socialization.

Public Schools Undermine Faith

Many Christian parents are concerned that homeschooling would not allow their children to fulfill the great commission of sharing the Gospel with nonbelievers. They often site Matthew 5:14–16 about being the light of the world.

Some Christian homeschool parents argue that even though young believers are to reach out to the lost, they are not called to immerse themselves daily in a hostile setting that constantly works to influence them in the ways of the world. They recognize that those with strong Christian upbringings are still vulnerable to the ungodly climate of the schools.

In Proverbs 4:11–15, King Solomon realized the vulnerability of his son, proclaiming his responsibility to train him in godly teachings and keep him from stumbling over the vices of this world.

Just as parents know that children are not prepared for war, many Christians believe that youth are not equipped to fend for themselves in the spiritual warfare taking place within schools.

A nationwide survey conducted by the Barna Group shows that 80 percent of Christian families send their children to public schools where their faith is attacked. Based on the study's findings, it appears that their kids are the ones being "evangelized" by the religion of secular humanism. More than half of their Christian teens believe Jesus actually sinned and only nine percent hold to moral absolutes, while 83 percent of children from committed Christian families attending public schools adopt a Marxist-Socialist worldview, reports the group.

Consistent with these figures, Christian producer and occult expert Caryl Matrisciana reports that 75 percent of public-schooled American youth brought up in Christian households disown their Christian faith by the first year of college. NHERI finds that this is only true for less than four percent of homeschooled youth.

Most home educators would not trade the blessings that homeschooling brings their families and society for the world.

"*Children who are educated at home but are not known to the local authority may be more likely to be at risk.*"

Homeschoolers May Be at Greater Risk for Child Abuse

Graham Badman

Graham Badman was the former director of Children's Services at Kent County Council in Britain. In the following viewpoint, he argues that, because they are less likely to come into contact with a range of adults, child abuse of homeschooled children is more likely to go unnoticed than child abuse of others. To address this, Badman recommends giving child welfare agencies more authority to monitor homeschool students. He also suggests that authorities should have the power to deny the right to homeschool in cases where there may be a danger of abuse.

As you read, consider the following questions:

1. The National Association of Social Workers in Education expresses concern because legislation only makes it possible to consider what in evaluating homeschooling families?

Graham Badman, *Report to the Secretary of State on the Review of Elective Home Education in England.* London, United Kingdom: The Stationery Office, 2009. © Crown copyright 2009. Reproduced by permission.

2. Badman recommends that local authorities should report homeschooling households on what grounds?

3. According to Badman, does evidence exist that home education is a factor in the forced marriages or trafficking of children?

Of all the matters considered during the course of this inquiry [into home education in Britain] the question of safeguarding electively home educated children has prompted the most vociferous response. Many parents have expressed anger and outrage that it was suggested that elective home education could be used as a cover for abuse. They have not been slow to point out that the most dangerous and damaging abuse of children is often before statutory school age or where children have been withdrawn from school or are already known to children's social care.

Causes for Concern

Many home educators argue that press coverage of this review has cast them as "guilty" with a need to prove "innocence" just by virtue of being a home educator. And many have argued for a measured response to prevent "hard cases becoming bad law". In addressing this issue I have tried to answer two fundamental questions:

- First, if there is abuse of children within the home education community, is it disproportionately high, relative to the general population?

- Secondly, where abuse does exist, would a change of regulation with regard to elective home education have either prevented or ameliorated such abuse?

It would be wrong to assume that home educators do not take the question of child safety, their own and others, very seriously. Some home educators who contributed to this review argued for periodic spot checks by authorities. The view was also expressed that attendance at school was no guarantee of a child's safety, as other tragic cases have indicated.

I understand the argument but do not accept it in its entirety in that attendance at school brings other eyes to bear, and does provide opportunity for the child to disclose to a trusted adult. Furthermore the 2004 Children Act, with its emphasis upon five outcomes for children including their safety not just their achievement, places new responsibilities upon schools to work with other agencies in a preventative way.

Some home educators have access to support and guidance from their organisations on recognising and dealing with child protection and many in conversation stressed to me the importance of their informal networks and knowledge of their own community. I am not persuaded that, although laudable, this is sufficient. Apart from which, on the basis of local authority responses to my questionnaire, there are many children likely to be unknown to the authorities or engaged in such networks. . . .

Isolated Children May Be Endangered

In seeking to answer the two questions posed earlier I have sought evidence and advice from protecting services and a range of third sector and other agencies that are engaged in the promotion of child safety and the protection of children. I have also analysed recent serious case reviews and sought information from local authorities on the number of electively home educated children subject to a child protection plan or were previously on the Child Protection Register.

The NSPCC [National Society for the Prevention of Cruelty to Children] is quite clear in its response in seeking a registration scheme and changed guidance.

"We do not agree that the status quo should be maintained and do think that monitoring should be strengthened. We are concerned that the child's safety and welfare should be paramount and that there is nothing in the current guidance or framework that would prevent children from being abused by people who may claim to be home educators. The current guidance on EHE [elective home education] says that the local authority can investigate if they have a concern about the child's education, but they do not have the powers to visit or meet the child. The guidance (paragraph 2.15) refers to the ability to see a child under s47 of the Children Act 1989. In order for a professional to use s47 they 'must have reasonable cause to suspect that a child who lives or is found in their area is suffering, or likely to suffer, significant harm'. If a child who is being abused is not afforded opportunities outwith [outside] the house, then the slim chances of them being identified become even smaller than they already are. In such a situation, because there is no education concern, the local authority does not investigate, as there are no grounds to do so. If a member of the public sees the child (and this would need to be regularly) then they are unlikely to contact an appropriate body. It then becomes a catch-22 as no concern is raised, because the child or the environment in which they are cared for is not seen."

The National Children's Bureau . . . [has] raised similar concerns.

The National Association of Social Workers in Education (NASWE) is more equivocal in its response but recognises the difficulty for local authorities under existing guidance to exercise their duty of care.

"The lack of regulation has made it very difficult for local authorities to exercise their duty of care to the child or young person concerned and may compromise a child's right to education. The legislation only makes it possible to consider the *education* on offer and this goes against all other aspects of their work with children.. . . . EHE is not in itself a safeguarding issue although the failure to provide a satisfactory education (in any context) may seriously compromise a child's future opportunities. EHE removes the opportunity for what is a very efficient method for monitoring and surveillance through attendance at school. Consequently the issue of EHE has become conflated with safeguarding concerns which may exist regardless of the method by which a child receives education."

Regulatory Change Is Needed

Her Majesty's Chief Inspector (HMCI) [in Britain, the Chief Inspector of Education monitors and reports on educational matters], in her submission, makes it clear that irrespective of the number of cases, change in regulation is necessary, furthermore that there is an unacceptable variation in the practice of local authorities and Local Safeguarding Children Boards (LSCBs) [local bodies of representatives from all main child welfare agencies in a given town, city, or region]:

"Our experience from inspections of children's services and evaluations of serious case reviews is that there is variation across the country in how proactively local safeguarding children boards ensure these children are safeguarded. Some local child protection procedures address this robustly while others do not. Current DCSF [Department for Children, Schools, and Families] guidelines for local authorities on elective home education place insufficient emphasis on safeguarding the welfare of children. In a small number of cases, our evaluation of serious case reviews has identified that a lack of oversight of children receiving home education contributed to a serious incident or the death of a child. Schools have an important responsibility to monitor children's safety and welfare, but this safety net is missing for children educated at home. In addition, children who are educated at home may have less access to trusted adults who they can turn to if they are concerned about their home circumstances."

Ofsted [Office for Standards in Education, Children's Services and Skills] go on to report findings from a small study they conducted in 2008 into the effectiveness of local authority policies to manage the risks to children who are not attending school nor receiving education elsewhere.

"Some authorities expressed the view that securing adequate safeguarding would be easier if they had a clear right of access to family homes in the course of monitoring the suitability of home education. Some authorities reported that national organisations for home education were advising parents to deny access to officers from children's services who were attempting to establish the suitability of the provision. Ofsted is concerned that this advice may increase the risk of harm to some children. Children who are educated at home but are not known to the local authority may be more likely to be at risk. Local authorities are notified when children are removed from local authority school rolls. However, during the survey referred to above, five local authorities expressed concern that some independent schools in their area did not notify them when pupils were taken off roll."

More Monitoring

In the light of the submission by HMCI and the other evidence, I recommend:

That the Children's Trust Board ensures that the Local Safeguarding Children Board (LSCB) reports to them on an annual basis with regard to the safeguarding provision and actions taken in relation to home educated children. This report shall also be sent to the National Safeguarding Delivery Unit. Such information should be categorised thereby avoiding current speculation with regard to the prevalence of child protection concerns amongst home educated children which may well be exaggerated. This information should contribute to and be contained within the National Annual Report.

United Kingdom Restricts Homeschooling Based on Badman Report

Ministers today unveiled plans for a major toughening-up of the regulation of home education, forcing families who opt out of schooling to register annually with their local authorities, submit learning plans and undergo regular inspections. If they fail the inspections they could be made to send their children to school.

The plans, contained in an independent report [by Graham Badman], . . . were ordered to address concerns that home education has been used as a cover for child abuse.

Polly Curtis,
"Government Moves to Tighten Regulation of Home Education,"
Guardian, *June 11, 2009. www.guardian.co.uk.*

To return to the two questions posed earlier. First, on the basis of local authority evidence and case studies presented, even acknowledging the variation between authorities, the number of children known to children's social care in some local authorities is disproportionately high relative to the size of their home educating population. Secondly, despite the small number of serious case reviews where home education was a feature, the consideration of these reviews and the data outlined above suggest that those engaged in the support and monitoring of home education should be alert to the potential additional risk to children. So saying is not to suggest that there is a causal or determining relationship, but simply an indication of the need for appropriately trained and knowledgeable personnel. To that end, I recommend:

That those responsible for monitoring and supporting home education, or commissioned so to do, are suitably qualified and experienced to discharge their duties and responsibilities set out in *Working Together to Safeguard Children* [an official 2006 publication of DCSF] to refer to social care services children who they believe to be in need of services or where there is reasonable cause to suspect that a child is suffering, or is likely to suffer, significant harm.

That local authority adult services and other agencies be required to inform those charged with the monitoring and support of home education of any properly evidenced concerns that they have of parents' or carers' ability to provide a suitable education irrespective of whether or not they are known to children's social care, on such grounds as:

- alcohol or drug abuse

- incidents of domestic violence

- previous offences against children

And in addition:

- anything else which may affect their ability to provide a suitable and efficient education.

This requirement should be considered in the Government's revision of *Working Together to Safeguard Children* Guidance.

Authorities May Prevent Home Schooling

Local authorities have a general duty, when carrying out functions in the education context, to safeguard and promote the welfare of children. Provision for the protection of children is contained in the Children Act 1989 and includes [a] provision that local authorities have a duty to investigate where they have reasonable cause to suspect that a child in their area is suffering or is likely to suffer significant harm. Whether a child may or may not have already come to the attention of the local authority because of safeguarding concerns, I believe it is of crucial importance in any registration scheme to give the local authority a discretion to prevent a child being electively home educated for safeguarding reasons. I therefore recommend:

> That the DCSF make such change as is necessary to the legislative framework to enable local authorities to refuse registration on safeguarding grounds. In addition, local authorities should have the right to revoke registration should safeguarding concerns become apparent.

With regard to other specific groups within the remit of this inquiry I can find no evidence that elective home education is a particular factor in the removal of children to forced marriage, servitude or trafficking or for inappropriate abusive activities. Based on the limited evidence available, this view is supported by the Association of Chief Police Officers. That is not to say that there are not isolated cases of trafficking that have been brought to my attention.

The foregoing would confirm my view that had there been different regulations in place as proposed, they may well have had a mitigating effect without necessarily guaranteeing prevention. However, any regulation is only as effective as its transaction. To that end I believe it is important to hold local authorities to account, identify and disseminate good practice and ensure that in addition to the training proposed earlier, that local authority and other staff are adequately and properly trained in safeguarding procedures and requirements.

> *"There are no statistics to prove that home-schooled children are more likely than public-schooled children to suffer unobserved abuse."*

Homeschooling Is Not Linked to Child Abuse

Jodie Gilmore

Jodie Gilmore is principal at Fulcrum Communications and a columnist for the New American. *In the following viewpoint, Gilmore argues that homeschoolers face many obstacles, such as anti-homeschooling bills, media smears, and the accusation of hidden child abuse. Claiming that homeschooling is just a mask for child abuse is just one of the many ways the media have recently tried to discredit the alternative form of education. Gilmore ultimately concludes that child abuse occurs in all types of families—both with homeschooled and public-schooled children. Homeschooling does not cause child abuse.*

As you read, consider the following questions:

1. On what three issues do anti-homeschooling bills generally focus, according to the viewpoint?

2. According to Gilmore, is there a causal relationship between homeschooling and abuse?

3. As stated in the viewpoint, what facts did the *Akron Beacon Journal's* article fail to state?

Thomas Jefferson once said that the "price of freedom is eternal vigilance." That has never been more true than in the case of the freedom to homeschool in the U.S. In the '80s and '90s, a battle was fought in the courtrooms and legislatures of this country, and by 1993, it was legal to homeschool in all 50 states. It was a hard-won battle, and there continues to be guerrilla warfare at work to reverse the victory. Homeschool proponents must eternally watch for laws and regulations seeking to restrict and control home schooling, must constantly rebut media attacks on home schooling, and continually educate home-schoolers about issues that can undermine the home-schooling movement.

Opponents of home schooling use several methods when trying to weaken or eradicate home schooling: legislative and regulatory actions, media smears, and subtle attempts to blur the line between public schooling and home schooling to exert more control over home-schoolers. This admittedly clever three-pronged approach is thorough—enact anti-home-schooling laws where possible, discredit home-schoolers with the general public, and confuse home-schoolers themselves.

But a well-educated citizenry can see through these various charades and work to stop them before they do any harm. A few examples of each kind of attack illustrate the basic form the home schooling conflict takes.

Direct Legislation and Regulation

When anti-home-schooling bills or regulations are proposed in a state legislature or an education department, they often center around three popular issues: compulsory attendance age, approval or control of the curriculum, and standardized testing.

With concerted effort, home-schoolers can meet and defeat these challenges to their educational freedom. For example, this year Montana introduced what HSLDA [Home School Legal Defense Association] called the "worst bill of the decade." Senate Bill 291 would have required home schools to be supervised by a certified teacher and monitored biannually by the school district, prohibited the home schooling of any child with developmental disabilities (despite the existence of many studies proving that special needs students learn better in a home-school setting), and prohibited home schooling by stepparents and legal guardians.

Outraged by the bill, Montana home-schoolers and the HSLDA lobbied extensively against the bill. Some 1,200 Montanans showed up for the Senate education committee hearing on the bill, at which the bill was permanently tabled. Senator Don Ryan (D-Great Falls), who sponsored the bill, said his bill was designed to prevent abusive and neglectful parents from hiding their children from authorities. But Montana Senate Minority Leader Bob Keenan (R-Bigfork) called S.B. 291 "a legislative assault on families and freedom."

Sometimes victories can be won with little effort by individuals who are knowledgeable. On May 27, the attendance officer for the Gilroy, Calif., Unified School District, Frank Valadez, stated in a letter to the editor in the *Gilroy Dispatch* that home educators must seek approval from the district attendance officer before they school their children at home— and if approval is not granted, the family will be referred to the School Attendance Review Board (SARB). And if SARB determines the child's education is not "adequate," the child will be considered truant.

However, [J.] Michael Smith, president of the HSLDA, responded to Valadez's letter, stating that in California, home educators are "small private schools in the home" and therefore home education in California is not subject to approval or evaluation by the local school district. "There is no authority for public school officials to evaluate, approve, or verify that the private school is providing an adequate education to the children enrolled in it."

The government also persecutes home-schoolers via social workers. Social workers violate the Fourth Amendment by claiming parents rights don't apply during a child-abuse investigation. In the 1999 case *Calabretta v. Floyd*, the United States Court of Appeals for the Ninth Circuit held that social workers, or policemen in support of social workers, are not exempt from the requirements of the Fourth Amendment. But social workers continue to ignore home-schoolers' rights.

In 2003, a social worker showed up at the door of an Enid, Oklahoma, home-schooling residence, citing a report that the children were not fed properly and there was no food in the house—and demanded entry into the house. The mother called HSLDA, and, following their advice, refused the social worker entry. She then brought armloads of food out and laid them on the front porch at the social worker's feet. Before the pile got very big, the social worker conceded that there appeared to be food, and left.

Media Smears

In the mid-'90s, journalists used to cry, "Oh, the poor home-schooled child—he'll get no socialization!" The socialization theory has been proven wrong, however. For example, a 2004 study, funded by the National Home Education Research Institute and called "Home Educated and Now Adults," concluded that "Based on the findings of this study, the concerns . . . that home schooling would somehow interfere with home-educated adults participating in essential societal activities or that homeschooling inhibits public debate, have no foundation." A book by Susan [A.] McDowell, *But What About So-*

cialization? Answering the Perpetual Home Schooling Question: A Review of the Literature, presents an exhaustive analysis of 24 studies on the socialization of home-schoolers, concluding: "It's a non-issue today." McDowell is the founder and president of Philodeus Press and is editor of the academic, refereed journal, *Home School Researcher*.

Undeterred, the media have recently chosen alternative ways to discredit home schooling. The most common theme is child safety—equating home schooling with child abuse in the minds of uncritical readers. For example, a 2002 article "Flaws in Home Schooling Exposed" in the *Independent Journal* portrayed an especially awful situation of child abuse, polygamy and murder, and then cited freedom to home educate as a major contributing factor in the case. More recently, based on accusations against a home schooling Florida family, many newspapers across the nation have published articles calling for increased regulation of home schooling because it "facilitates child abuse."

Major television shows have also jumped on the home-schooling/child-abuse bandwagon. In 2003, CBS news aired a series about the "dark side" of home schooling, and in 2004, *Law & Order: Special Victims Unit* featured a home-school child abuse story.

But when parents of publicly schooled children commit child abuse, the same media sources do not insinuate that there is a causal relationship between public schooling and the crime (which of course, there isn't—any more than there is a causal relationship between home schooling and child abuse). Regrettably, child abuse occurs in all types of families, both home-schooled and public-schooled.

Critics of home schooling say that abuse is easier to hide in the home-school environment, but there are no statistics to prove that home-schooled children are more likely than public-schooled children to suffer unobserved abuse. As Sarah A. McUmber-House, a veteran home-schooler, points out, it would make as much sense to blame the mail-order industry, or the clothing industry, or the makeup industry for child abuse—each of these industries could support an "isolationist" lifestyle and make products that could cover up signs of abuse.

"I suggest we all learn to recognize the difference between a related detail, and a causal detail. Yes, homeschooling is a related detail in these stories, but it is not a causal detail," said McUmber-House.

Lack of logic, however, rarely bothers mainstream media sources. As a prime example, the *Akron Beacon Journal* [in Ohio] published in November 2004 a series of seven articles that cast home schooling in a negative light. The authors conceded that home schooling had some good points, but also implied that increased government oversight was required to fix some of home schooling's dangerous flaws.

However, as pointed out by Nathaniel and Hans Bluedorn (home-schooled authors of a logic textbook, *The Fallacy Detective*), the *Beacon* articles use flawed logic and statistics. The Bluedorns point out errors of logic occurring in the *Beacon* articles, including appealing to unspecified, uncertified, unverified sources; using a lack of evidence as proof; and using manipulative language.

The *Beacon*'s use of statistics was poor, as well. For example, the authors stated that despite the fact that about two percent of the U.S. student population is home-schooled, less than 0.2 percent of college applicants are home-schooled. The authors fail to mention that, because of the rapid growth of the home-schooling movement in the last decade, the vast majority of home-schooled children are less than 14 years old—and are therefore hardly ready to apply to college. An article called "Let the Facts Speak," by the HSLDA, further elaborates on this fallacy: some states consider home schools to be "private schools"; therefore, those states' colleges would bunch home-schooled applicants in with "privately schooled applicants."

Keep Up the Good Work

The fact that home schooling is under siege actually has a silver lining: if home schooling weren't working; if it weren't growing; if it weren't turning out a brand new generation of leaders who have sound minds, good values, a strong work ethic, and a commitment to independence, then the Establishment wouldn't be working so hard to derail the home-schooling movement. And the Establishment is finding that derailment hard to accomplish, thanks to the momentum gained by the home-schooling movement on all fronts.

Periodical Bibliography

The following articles have been selected to supplement the diverse views presented in this chapter.

Daniel Bates — "Home Schooling 'Could Be a Cover for Child Abuse and Sex Exploitation,'" *Daily Mail Online*, January 20, 2009. www.dailymail.co.uk.

Chris Klicka — "Socialization: Homeschoolers Are in the Real World," Home School Legal Defense Association (HSLDA), March 2007. www.hslda.org.

Robert Kunzman — "An Army of Home-Schooled 'Christian Soldiers' on a Mission to 'Take Back America for God,'" AlterNet, September 7, 2009. www.alternet.org.

Dan Lips and Evan Feinberg — "Homeschooling: A Growing Option in American Education," *Backgrounder* (The Heritage Foundation), no. 2122, April 3, 2008. www.heritage.org.

Carole Moore — "Why Homeschooling Isn't Right for Us," Scholastic.com. www2.scholastic.com.

Isabel Shaw — "Social Skills and Homeschooling: Myths and Facts," FamilyEducation.com. http://school.familyeducation.com.

Ian Slatter — "New Nationwide Study Confirms Homeschool Academic Achievement," Home School Legal Defense Association (HSLDA), August 10, 2009. www.hslda.org.

Tammy Takahashi — "Gender Roles and Socialization in School and Homeschooling," Just Enough and Nothing More Blog, April 22, 2009. www.justenoughblog.com.

Paul Viggiano — "Homeschool Ruling Reveals Educational Double Standard," *Daily Breeze Online*, October 4, 2009. www.dailybreeze.com.

CHAPTER 2

How Should Homeschooling Be Regulated?

Chapter Preface

Within the homeschooling community, one of the most controversial regulatory initiatives has been the Homeschool Non-Discrimination Act (HONDA). The act was originally proposed in 2003 and was strongly backed by the Home School Legal Defense Association (HSLDA), one of the most important nationwide homeschooling organizations. In a July 2003 post on its Web site, the HSLDA explained, "There are currently several areas of federal law that unfairly impact home education. Congress must pass the Homeschool Non-Discrimination Act (HONDA) to remedy this unfair treatment." HONDA would, according to HSLDA, make it easier for homeschooled students to receive financial aid, make it easier for homeschooled students to work outside the home, make homeschooled students eligible for certain scholarships, and address other areas in which homeschooled students are at a disadvantage compared to students in public and private schools.

HONDA did not pass the House of Representatives in 2003, but it was reintroduced in 2005 along with a new provision making it easier for homeschoolers to enlist in the military. The new provision—and, indeed, the whole idea of federal legislation regarding homeschoolers—was opposed by many people within the homeschooling community. For example, commenter Deborah Stevenson, quoted by writer Ann Zeise in an October 10, 2005, post on the blog A to Z Home's Cool, stated, "While the intent of the bill may be honorable, the effect of the bill is potentially disastrous for homeschooling parents who want to remain free from government regulation. This is because the federal government has no constitutional authority to directly regulate the education of homeschooled students, whether that regulation is for the benefit of the students or not." Valerie Moon, writing on the

Web site of *Home Education Magazine*, called the new military provisions of HONDA "useless" and said that "the paper [HONDA] is written on should be burnt."

HONDA elicited such powerful emotions in part because it touched on some of the most strongly held beliefs of the homeschooling movement. Homeschoolers, who have deliberately decided to avoid state schools, are often very wary of any sort of federal interference in their children's education.

As of early 2010, HONDA has still not passed, and it seems unlikely to do so in the near future. The following viewpoints, however, will look at a number of other regulatory issues that continue to confront homeschoolers.

> "States must—not may or should—
> regulate homeschooling to ensure that
> parents provide their children with a
> basic constitutionally mandated mini-
> mum education."

Homeschooling Should Be Regulated by the Government

Kimberly A. Yuracko

Kimberly A. Yuracko is a professor of law at Northwestern University School of Law. In the following viewpoint, she argues that the U.S. government has a constitutional obligation to ensure a minimum level of education for all children. She also argues that the power and right to educate the child comes first from the state, not from the parent. Therefore, she concludes, homeschooling needs to be much more closely regulated to ensure that all parents, especially conservative religious parents, are meeting the legal educational requirements.

As you read, consider the following questions:

1. In the early 1980s, homeschooling was illegal in what part of the United States, according to Yuracko?

Kimberly A. Yuracko, "Education off the Grid: Constitutional Constraints on Home-schooling," *96 California Law Review 123* (2008). © 2008 by the California Law Review, Inc. Reprinted from California Law Review vol. 96, No. 1, by permission of the Regents of the University of California and the author.

2. According to Yuracko, the Home School Legal Defense Association's commitment to ensuring parents' unfettered right to homeschool rests on what two core ideological beliefs?

3. In *Marsh v. Alabama,* did the Supreme Court find that it was or was not legal for a company-owned town to prevent a Jehovah's Witness from distributing literature? What was the reasoning?

Ann and Bob Smith are a devoutly religious couple who choose to homeschool their seven-year-old twins Susan and Sam. In accordance with their religious beliefs, they teach their children only religious doctrine, refusing to provide their children with a basic education in reading, writing and arithmetic. The Smiths are permitted by the laws of their state to adopt such a plan. My guess is that the visceral response of many, if not most, readers is that a state simply cannot permit noneducation of this sort be it by state or private actors. The question is of more than academic importance. In response to strong lobbying from homeschoolers, states have increasingly deregulated homeschooling and relinquished any oversight and control.

Homeschooling and HSLDA

Homeschooling is no longer a "fringe" phenomenon. Homeschooling was common in the United States before the nineteenth century, but by the early 1980s the practice was illegal in most states. Since then, homeschooling has enjoyed a dramatic rebirth. Today, homeschooling is legal in all states. Estimates of the number of children currently homeschooled range from 1.1 to 2 million. The 1.1 million estimate represents 2.2 percent of the school-age population in the country. Even conservative estimates place the number of homeschooled children at twice the number of students enrolled in conservative Christian schools and more than the number of students enrolled in Wyoming, Alaska, Delaware, North Dakota, Vermont, South Dakota, Montana, Rhode Island, New Hampshire, and Hawaii—the ten lowest states in terms of student enrollment—combined. Moreover, scholars estimate that the number of children receiving their education through homeschooling is growing at a rate of ten to twenty percent per year. . . .

By the early 1990s, homeschooling had expanded and divided into two distinct movements: one secular and the other conservative Christian. Mitchell [L.] Stevens, who has performed the most extensive sociological study of contemporary homeschooling to date, explains: "[H]ome schoolers were divided into two quite different movement worlds. They read different publications, attended different support groups, and heeded different kinds of advice about how to act politically." These two factions were not, however, of equal size and strength. The Christian homeschooling movement came to dominate its secular counterpart in size, profile and political influence. In other words, while homeschoolers themselves continue to be a diverse lot, the homeschooling movement has become defined and driven by its conservative Christian majority.

At the heart of the Christian homeschooling movement is the Home School Legal Defense Association (HSLDA). HSLDA's commitment to ensuring parents' unfettered right to homeschool flows from two core ideological beliefs. The first is a belief in parental control—indeed ownership—of children. "Parental rights are under siege," HSLDA warns. "The basic fundamental freedom of parents to raise their children hangs in the balance. Have we forgotten whose children they are anyway? They are a God-given responsibility to parents," HSLDA proclaims. Indeed, Michael Farris, an HSLDA founder and its former president, argues that "[t]he right of parents to control the education of their children is so fundamental that it deserves the extraordinary level of protection as an absolute right." The second is a belief in the need for Christian families to separate and shield their children from harmful secular social values. Public schools, Farris cautions, have been "promoting values that are questionable or clearly wrong: the acceptability of homosexuality as an alternative lifestyle; the acceptability of premarital sex as long as it is 'safe'; the acceptability of relativistic moral standards." Such indoctrination, he argues, is "probably more dangerous to our ultimate freedom than armed enemies." Fortunately, according to Farris, the moral obligation to protect one's child from such indoctrination is protected by a constitutional right. "[P]arents have the constitutional right to obey the dictates of God concerning education of their children."

Pushing Deregulation

Motivated by these beliefs, HSLDA—along with the National Center for Home Education (NCHE), HSLDA's service arm designed to link, inform and organize state homeschool leaders, and the Congressional Action Program (CAP), HSLDA's lobbying organization—has become a powerful political force. For the last two decades HSLDA has opposed virtually all state oversight and regulation of homeschooling. The clout of HSLDA and its grassroots Christian activists is now well recognized in political circles. Indeed, in 2000 former U.S. Representative Bill Goodling from Pennsylvania, the former chair of the House Committee on Education and the Workforce [now the Committee on Education and Labor], called homeschoolers "the most effective educational lobby on Capitol Hill." . . .

In addition to preventing the passage of new state laws regulating homeschooling, HSLDA has effectively challenged existing state laws. Over the past 15 years, HSLDA has devoted its resources to challenging teacher certification requirements for homeschool teachers, subject matter requirements for homeschools, testing requirements for homeschooled children, and home inspection visits of homeschools. As a result of

HSLDA's work, state laws regulating homeschooling have become increasingly lenient. According to HSLDA, only twenty-five states presently require standardized testing and evaluation of homeschooled students. Moreover, ten states—those labeled by HSLDA as having the lowest regulation of homeschooling—do not even require homeschooling parents to notify the state of their intent to homeschool. For example, Alaska—one of the most explicitly hands-off states with regard to homeschooling—exempts homeschooled students from its compulsory education laws and imposes no subject matter or testing requirements on homeschooled students. "Homeschooling" of virtually any sort is legal under Alaska law. In short, oversight of homeschooling in several states is so lax as to be nonexistent. Moreover, the trend points toward even less state oversight and regulation of homeschooling. States are not only looking the other way when homeschoolers do not comply with state laws, but actually changing their laws to grant even greater freedom to homeschoolers.

Surprisingly, the social and legal implications of this phenomenon have received almost no scholarly attention. For decades political theorists have worried and argued about what steps a liberal society must take to protect children being raised in illiberal communities. They have focused their attention on the extent to which a liberal society must permit or condemn such practices as polygamy, clitoridectomy, and child marriage. Virtually absent from the debate has been any discussion of the extent to which a liberal society should condone or constrain homeschooling, particularly as practiced by religious fundamentalist families explicitly seeking to shield their children from liberal values of sex equality, gender role fluidity and critical rationality.

Constitutional Minimum Education

This [viewpoint] seeks to begin to fill this important void. It explores the constitutional limits that the state action doctrine

Testing for Home-Schoolers

Home-schooling regulations are only justified, [researcher Robert] Kunzman says, when (1) vital interests of children or society are at stake, (2) there is a general consensus on standards for meeting those interests, and (3) there is an effective way to measure whether those standards are met. Kunzman offers only one possible regulation that meets all three criteria: He thinks homeschoolers, like regular school children, should be tested for basic skills in reading, writing and math.

Jay Mathews,
"Three Smart Rules for Home School Regulation,"
Washington Post, *Class Struggle Blog, August 21, 2009.*
http://voices.washingtonpost.com/class-struggle.

places on states' ability to delegate unfettered control over education to homeschooling parents. . . . It argues that states must—not may or should—regulate homeschooling to ensure that parents provide their children with a basic constitutionally mandated minimum education. . . .

This argument about the constitutionally mandated minimum education that states must require of homeschools is critically important for two reasons. Conceptually, it rejects the dominant HSLDA view that parents possess absolute control over their children's education. It highlights the legal distinctness of parents and children and emphasizes that parental control over children's basic education flows from the state (rather than vice versa). States delegate power over children's basic education to parents, and the delegation itself is necessarily subject to constitutional constraints. Certainly there is an upper limit to states' control over children's education. Parents do have constitutionally protected liberty interests in their relationship with their children. This [viewpoint] does not address the upper limits on state regulation. What it emphasizes, however, is that there is a lower limit as well—a minimum level of regulation and oversight over children's education that states may not avoid. This lower limit belies the claim that parents have absolute educational control.

Practically, and perhaps more importantly, the argument demands that states bring homeschooling families into the regulatory structure. This demand is critical, even apart from concern over the quality of homeschool education. It means that homeschooling parents cannot separate themselves entirely from society; they cannot exist "off the grid." The required oversight puts a real as well as a symbolic break on anti-secular separatism. Moreover, it may, in turn, remind legislators of the area of discretion between the lower and upper bounds of state control over education wherein they wield significant power, thereby making normative discussions about the optimal level and type of education regulation both more likely and more useful. . . .

States Must Ensure Basic Education

Anecdotal evidence suggests that at least some homeschooled children, by design or accident, may not be receiving even a basic minimum education. The fact that one cannot know for sure how rare such occurrences are is itself a problem. I contend . . . as a matter of federal and state constitutional law, states may not permit such deprivation. . . .

While the question of whether there is a federal constitutional right to a basic minimum level of education remains unsettled, there is reason to believe that such a fundamental right does exist. Moreover, the existence of state constitutional rights to this effect is considerably more certain. . . .

For at least sixty years, education has been recognized as a core public function. Indeed, as the Supreme Court asserted in 1954 in *Brown v. Board of Education [of Topeka]*, "[E]ducation is perhaps the most important function of state and local governments." Moreover . . . it is one which entails, as a matter of state and perhaps also federal constitutional law, providing children with the opportunity for a basic minimum level of education.

To the extent that homeschooling parents control the public function of providing a basic minimum level of education, they are bound by the state's own constitutional obligations. . . .

Individuals Who Take State Power Must Be Regulated

The monopolistic power of the state and its ability to foreclose exit options for those who disagree with its policies are a core reason to impose constitutional restraints on state conduct, as opposed to private conduct. State policies bind all citizens and preclude conflicting private conduct. In contrast, when private parties act, both the scope of their power and the effect of their conduct are less severe. Private individuals are diverse and do not, as a rule, operate monopolistically. Private conduct is unlikely to be uniform or coherent. As a result, private conduct is unlikely to foreclose options in the same way or to the same degree that state action does.

When, however, private actors exercise monopolistic control over a traditionally public function, courts treat the private actor as if it were the state for the purposes of constitutional challenge. The private actor then becomes subject to the same federal and state constitutional obligations that bind the state in its performance of the public function.

Consider, for example, the Supreme Court's ruling in *Marsh v. Alabama*. *Marsh* raised the question of whether the company-owned town of Chickasaw, Alabama, could prohibit a Jehovah's Witness from distributing religious literature in the town. The plaintiff argued that such a prohibition violated her First and Fourteenth Amendment rights. In its analysis, the Court emphasized the company's monopolistic control over the town's streets and sidewalks, as well as the fact that the company was operating as a public entity normally would. Because of these facts, the Court treated the company's conduct as if it were state conduct and held that the company's conduct violated the plaintiff's First Amendment rights. The Court explained that "[w]hether a corporation or a municipality owns or possesses the town the public in either case has an identical interest in the functioning of the community in such manner that the channels of communication remain free." "The managers appointed by the corporation," the Court concluded, "cannot curtail the liberty of press and religion of these people consistently with the purposes of the constitutional guarantees." . . .

The Supreme Court has made clear that what is important for the public function doctrine is not only that the private actor control a public function but that it control a public function that has been "traditionally the *exclusive* prerogative of the state." This makes sense. When private entities supersede the state in controlling a public function exclusively and monopolistically, third parties no longer have diverse private options. They need constitutional protections to ensure access. Thus such private actors should be treated as state actors.

Certainly, education has never been the exclusive domain of the state. Private schooling preceded public education and continues to exist alongside it. Nonetheless, in the absence of state regulation, homeschooling parents do exercise precisely the kind of monopolistic control over education with which the public function doctrine is concerned. Homeschooling parents make all the decisions about what educational materials and messages their children will be exposed to. Moreover, particularly for young children, there are no exit options. Young children do not have the power to bypass their parents' educational decisions and pursue different educational paths. Homeschooling parents, in short, exercise exclusive control over education, not with respect to all children, but with respect to their own children. As a result, they are appropriately bound by the state's own educational obligations.

> *"The same education bureaucrats who . . . achieve previously unknown levels of semi-literacy and illiteracy among otherwise normal American children feel compelled . . . to abandon their diligent pursuit of intellectual mediocrity to offer proposals for regulating homeschool parents."*

Homeschooling Should Not Be Regulated by the Government

Bruce N. Shortt

Bruce N. Shortt is a lawyer, a homeschooling parent, and the author of The Harsh Truth About Public Schools. *In the following viewpoint, he argues that public schools fail to educate children and that it is therefore ridiculous for the same school bureaucracies to demand to regulate homeschoolers. Shortt maintains that no evidence exists to suggest that un-credentialed homeschool parents hurt their children's education, nor that homeschool students are poorly socialized. In fact, Shortt argues, homeschool students consistently perform better than public school students, both academically and socially.*

As you read, consider the following questions:

1. Who is the superintendent of Mississippi public schools?

2. According to Shortt, what percentage of Mississippi's fourth graders cannot read at grade level?

3. According to Greg Cizek, what do researchers know about the socialization question?

In their never-ending effort to "help" homeschoolers, public school bureaucrats periodically try to increase homeschooling regulations. This makes K–12 education perhaps a unique endeavor: It's a field in which the failures regularly, and astonishingly, insist that they should be able to regulate the successful.

The Incompetent Regulating the Competent

Never mind that homeschoolers consistently outperform children institutionalized in government schools or that the longer a child is institutionalized in a government school the worse he does in relation to homeschooled children. Never mind, also, that international surveys of academic performance show that in the course of 12 years government schools manage to turn perfectly capable children into world-class dullards. No, the same education bureaucrats who consume an annual cash flow of roughly $600 billion to achieve previously unknown levels of semi-literacy and illiteracy among otherwise normal American children feel compelled from time to time to abandon their diligent pursuit of intellectual mediocrity to offer proposals for regulating homeschool parents.

The latest outbreak of education bureaucrat compassion comes from Mississippi. There the Grand Panjandrum, indeed, the very Mikado of Mississippi education, Superintendent Hank Bounds, is working at creating a panel of Quisling [a term used to describe traitors] homeschool parents to determine whether homeschool families should be further regulated.

Why does the estimable Superintendent Bounds think that homeschooled children would benefit from more attention from Mississippi's crack team of government educators? Well, because he worries that some parents might take their children out of government schools and then fail to educate them. As Bounds inarticulately put it in a November news conference:

> " ... [Y]ou must realize we all have this moral and ethical responsibility to deal with those situations where clearly it's nothing more than a child abuse situation when parents pull their children out of school, say they're being home-schooled just because parents ... don't want to be involved in the education of their children. ..."

Subsequently, the editorial staff of Jackson's *Clarion-Ledger* came to Bounds's aid by translating this gibberish into English. Evidently, Bounds and his *Clarion-Ledger* cheerleaders think that Mississippi parents are removing their children from Mississippi's government schools just so that they can deny them an education at home.

The State, Not the Home, Denies Education

Interestingly, neither Bounds nor the *Clarion-Ledger* point to any evidence that this is a significant problem in Mississippi or anywhere else. In fact, a little reflection would indicate that this expression of "concern" is more than a little disingenuous. After all, if you really don't want your children to be educated, the most effective strategy is to institutionalize them in one of Superintendent Bounds's government schools. That obviously requires much less effort than keeping them at home.

Moreover, if Bounds really wants to characterize a failure to educate as "child abuse," then what is to be said of him and his bureaucrats who are responsible for a school system in which a catastrophic failure to educate is the norm? According to the U.S. Department of Education's National Assessment of

Educational Progress, or NAEP, often known as "The Nation's Report Card," Bounds's bureaucrats have failed Mississippi's children and taxpayers as follows:

1. Reading: 82 percent of Mississippi's fourth graders cannot read at grade level, with *52 percent not being able to read at even a basic level.* By eighth grade, 82 percent of Mississippi's children still cannot read at grade level, with *40 percent being unable to read at even a basic level.*

2. Mathematics: 81 percent of fourth graders are below grade level in math, with 31 percent lacking even a basic grasp of mathematics. By eighth grade, math illiteracy is burgeoning in Mississippi: 86 percent of students are below grade level in math, with 48 percent lacking even a basic understanding of mathematics.

3. Science: 88 percent of fourth graders are below grade level, with 55 percent lacking even a basic knowledge of science. By eighth grade, 86 percent of Mississippi's children are below grade level, with an amazing 60 percent lacking a basic grasp of the subject.

Lest anyone be under the impression that the NAEP has unusually high academic standards, testimony before the Board of Governors for the NAEP indicates, for example, that the "advanced" mathematics questions for the eighth-grade NAEP are at best comparable to fifth-grade questions in Singapore's math curriculum. So, while the NAEP may not require high levels of academic competence, it does highlight Mississippi schools' systematic failure to educate.

And just where does the performance of Superintendent Bounds's Mississippi education bureaucracy put Mississippi's children nationally? Dead last in fourth-grade reading and eighth-grade math (tied with Alabama), and third from last in fourth-grade math and eighth-grade reading. Note that Bounds's schools manage to produce these prodigious levels of academic failure by spending roughly $7,000 per student per

---

Comparison of the National Average Percentile Scores of Homeschoolers and Public School Students

Based on a study commissioned by the Home School Legal Defense Association (HSLDA) of the results from 15 independent testing services.

Subtest	Homeschool	Public School
Reading	89	50
Language	84	50
Math	84	50
Science	86	50
Social Studies	84	50
Composite	86	50

TAKEN FROM: Ian Slatter, "New Nationwide Study Confirms Homeschool Academic Achievement," *HSLDA Website*, August 10, 2009. www.hslda.org.

---

year, an amount that would pay tuition at many, many excellent private schools. One shudders to think what Bounds's "educators" might accomplish with even more money.

Homeschoolers Are Not Disadvantaged

Apart from worrying about the possibility that a homeschooling parent somewhere might be lying in bed eating bonbons instead of teaching junior, Bounds and his editorial friends also fret about homeschooling parents who have not finished high school. With a little research, however, anyone, even including editorial writers, can discover that there is evidence indicating that *children homeschooled by parents without a high school diploma are at no disadvantage at all compared to public school students.*

As it turns out, in a basic battery of tests that included writing and mathematics, homeschooled children whose mothers hadn't finished high school scored in the 83rd percentile while students whose fathers hadn't finished high school scored in the 79th percentile. Bear in mind, too, that children in Mississippi public schools do not on average come close to doing this well on *any legitimate, nationally normed test*. Moreover, there are also studies that indicate that regulation does not have *any positive impact on the academic achievement levels* of homeschooled students.

Of course, no attack on homeschooling is complete without someone raising the "socialization" question. At least in this Bounds's pom-pom wavers at the *Clarion-Ledger* did not disappoint: "Can homeschooled children cope with social pressures, people skills? More is learned in a classroom and school setting than A-B-Cs. . . ."

Again, like the other "worries" deployed in scaring the public into supporting expanded homeschool regulation, a little research would have shown this to be a baseless concern. In 2001, Greg Cizek, associate professor of educational research at the University of North Carolina, summarized what researchers know about the "socialization" question: "It is basically a nonissue. . . . If anything, research shows that because parents are so sensitive to the charge, they expose them [their children] to so many activities." More recently, a study of 7,000 homeschooled adults found, among other things, much higher levels of civic involvement, participation in higher education, and life satisfaction among them than adults who were not homeschooled.

By attacking homeschool parents, Bounds is playing a familiar game. The goal is to distract the public's attention from the abject failure of the public schools for which he is responsible. After all, no government school system so thoroughly *fails* to educate as Bounds's schools. Nevertheless, Bounds wants the public to believe that the same bureaucrats who daily busy themselves producing massive illiteracy in Mississippi's public schools should have more power over homeschool parents, even though homeschooling parents are already doing a magnificent job with their children.

Perhaps we can all agree with Superintendent Bounds in one respect, however. Mississippi does need more regulation of education. Consequently, as a public service, here is my modest proposal for reforming Mississippi's public schools: Homeschooling parents should regulate Bounds until the students in the government schools for which he is responsible academically outperform homeschooled children. Unfortunately, this recommendation is not likely to be accepted, which means that state superintendents of education around the country will continue to be able to tell parents upset about the job their local schools are doing, "Well, at least we're not Mississippi."

> *"I [am not] aware of any studies show-ing that a person who is illiterate is better able to teach literacy than some-one who is literate."*

Homeschooling Parents Should Be Certified

Stephen Downes

Stephen Downes is a senior researcher for the National Research Council of Canada, specializing in the fields of online learning, new media, pedagogy, and philosophy. In the following view-point, he argues that homeschool parents must have basic quali-fications, such as the ability to read, if they are to teach their children. He maintains that a certification test for homeschool parents/teachers is necessary to make sure that students are not being denied a basic education.

As you read, consider the following questions:

1. According to Downes, do nations that score well in in-ternational tests employ alternative or uncertified in-structors?

Stephen Downes, "Homeschooling, Abuse and Qualifications," Halfanhour.blogspot .com, March 22, 2008. National Research Council of Canada. Reproduced by permis-sion.

2. According to Downes, parents are important in education not as teachers, but as what?

3. How many children died of abuse or neglect during federal fiscal year 2005, according to Downes?

[D]ana] Hanley [a homeschool parent and blogger] begins reasonably [in her blog post], stating [that] "no one is arguing that it is better [for homeschool parents] to not be certified." But then she asserts that "certification itself is an ineffective predictor of teacher ability and that research shows that there is no statistically significant difference between classroom teachers who are certified via the traditional route, via alternative certification programs and who enter the classroom uncertified."

Certification Is Better

On the whole, this assertion is implausible. While we agree that certified plumbers may be incompetent, and that uncertified plumbers may be competent, on the whole, in general, we take certification to be a reliable indicator of competence. And this belief is reflected in our behaviour: On the whole, we opt for certified plumbers, certified dentists, and certified doctors.

As evidence, Hanley cites a study of certified, uncertified, and alternatively certified teachers in New York City schools. One would have thought that a more general study would have been relevant, rather than a very focused look at a small number of teachers in one particular environment. A study, perhaps, such as Kate Walsh's *Teacher Certification Reconsidered: Stumbling for Quality*, published through the Abell Foundation. But this, I guess, would mean acknowledging the many studies that *do* assert that certification makes a difference. And it would mean responding to Linda Darling-Hammond's extended critique of the report.

We would expect some studies to show that certification is an unreliable indicator. But the study Hanley cites is not one of them. The authors state, "On average, the certification status of a teacher has at most small impacts on student test performance." And they admit that the subjects of the study are people who have been selected; they are highly motivated and educated. They are therefore not representative of the much wider population that is not certified.

My own view regarding certification accords with Darling-Hammond's:

> Certification is but a proxy for the subject matter knowledge and knowledge of teaching and learning embodied in various kinds of course work and in the evidence of ability to practice contained in supervised student teaching. It is true that certification is a relatively crude measure of teachers' knowledge and skills, since the standards for subject matter and teaching knowledge embedded in certification have varied across states and over time, are differently measured, and are differently enforced from place to place. . . . Given the crudeness of the measure, it is perhaps remarkable that so many studies have found significant effects of teacher certification.

Qualifications Are Vital

I am rather more interested in the *qualifications*, rather than the certification, of the person educating the learner. As Darling-Hammond states, certification is but a proxy. And as I have written elsewhere, I expect the larger community to contribute to the education of a child. This will necessarily involve people who are not certified as teachers—but on no account should it involve people who are *unqualified.*

I know of no research that suggests that a person untrained in carpentry would be as able to teach carpentry as someone who has been trained as a carpenter. Nor am I aware of any studies showing that a person who is illiterate is better able to teach literacy than someone who is literate. Teacher

State Qualifications for Home School Parents

Forty-one states do not require home school parents to meet any specific teacher qualifications. Those requiring a high school diploma or GED [general equivalency diploma] are Georgia, New Mexico, North Carolina, Ohio, Pennsylvania, South Carolina, and Tennessee. [North Dakota and West Virginia have additional requirements.]

Christopher J. Klicka,
"Summary of Home School Laws in the 50 States,"
School Reform News, *February 2005.*
www.heartland.org.

certification allows us to get some handle on those—and other—qualifications. It is by no means perfect, and 'alternative certification' even less so. But it is demonstrably better than nothing.

If parents are not even going to subject themselves to a literacy test—something that would be important, given the levels of functional illiteracy in the United States—then how can we know they are even able to teach their children to read.

Perhaps the best evidence comes from the international studies. . . . Nations that score well in international tests do not employ 'alternative' and uncertified instructors; quite the contrary. As Lisa Moore reports in *U.S. News & World Report*, "Perhaps the most potent secret weapon in Finland's success is well-trained teachers. In 1970, as the country began to overhaul its system, it mandated that teachers for all grades must obtain at least a master's degree. Today, teacher-education programs at universities are highly competitive, in part because teachers enjoy high prestige in Finnish society."

Parental Involvement

Hanley follows up her discussion of certification with an alternative theory: "I think it is important to note here that the only factor proven to have a significant effect on student performance beyond all socioeconomic factors is parental involvement." . . .

Hanley continues, "Parents are vital to the educational success of their children, and any system or solution we propose needs to take this into account."

I wish Hanley were more precise with what she means by "vital"—because we know that orphans are able to succeed educationally, as are children raised by guardians or even educated in (some) residential schools (such as Eton [a prestigious boarding school for thirteen- to nineteen-year-old boys]).

My own understanding—based on research such as is summarized by the Harvard Family Research Project—is that parents are important not so much as teachers but as role models, "such as reading and communicating with one's child, and the more subtle aspects of parental involvement, such as parental style and expectations."

In fact, even Hanley seems to agree that the *teaching* that takes place in homeschooling is almost incidental to its success:

> This is also the real reason why homeschoolers have traditionally been quite successful academically and socially after graduation. There is no magic formula; it is just that homeschooling selects for the most involved parents.

This may well be. But at the same time, this—and the research cited—suggests that some parents may play a significantly *negative* role in their children's education: parents who are not involved in their education, who do not (or cannot) read to their children, who have limited, or negative, expectations of their children.

Hanley writes, "it is just that homeschooling selects for the most involved parents." Perhaps. But it may also select for any number of other types of parents—including, for example, the abusive parents at the center of the court case that spawned this discussion.[1]

We cannot depend on some mysterious 'self-selection' mechanism to defend children against parents who would use the cover of homeschooling to perpetuate the sort of abuse cited in the court case. We need some sort of evaluation, some sort of assessment. Something that would indicate to us, incidentally, that the 'involved' parent can also fill some of the functions of the teachers they are replacing.

Certification seems like a very small requirement, for such high stakes.

Self-Selection Is Not Sufficient

There is an old adage: The law is made for other people. This applies in this case.

Hanley agrees with me that "many parents are simply not qualified to teach their own children. They lack a proper knowledge base, capacity for reason and any grounding in pedagogy or communication theory."

But then she asks:

> What has that to do with homeschooling? I know many competent adults who have graduated from college who say they could never teach their own children. While I think many of them could if they let go of some of their schoolish notions of what education means, it still points to a fundamental aspect of homeschooling rarely considered in these discussions: Homeschooling is self-regulating. Most people do not and will never try it . . . most will not even ever seri-

---

1. The case is *Jonathan L. and Mary Grace L. v. Superior Court of the State of California for the County of Los Angeles.* Decided in 2008, the case placed serious restrictions on homeschooling in California.

ously consider it. And many of those who do begin home-schooling find it too difficult and seek out other options for their children.

Quite so. Many people do not try homeschooling.

But it simply *does not follow* that the only people who try homeschooling are those who are qualified for it.

Some people are manifestly not qualified to offer home-schooling. The subjects of this court case offer an example of this.

Hanley is using a logic that only applies to people like her:

So long as the parent-child relationship is healthy, no one wants to see that child succeed more than the parent. Thus the parent who is failing at educating their own child will seek alternatives.

The problem is, there is a certain number of parent-child relationships that are *not* healthy. "During FFY [federal fiscal year, a period extending from October 1 to September 30] 2005, an estimated 1,460 children died due to child abuse or neglect." A certain number of parents who will *not* seek alter-natives, even if they are failing. A certain number of parents who will not even be able to recognize *that* they are failing.

The law must be made, not just for you, but for those other people. We need to know that you are *not* one of those people. 1,460 children died due to child abuse or neglect. Is it too much to ask for *some* guarantee that your children will not be among those statistics?

▌ *"Homeschooling parents, many of whom have declared their homes private schools, say what they do is legal."*

Homeschooling Parents Do Not Need to Be Certified

John Stossel

John Stossel is the co-anchor for ABC News's 20/20. In the following viewpoint, he argues that a California appellate court ruling that parents have no constitutional right to educate their children at home may be unfair. The education code is vague and does not specifically address homeschooling. While there are claims that a parent should not be able to homeschool their child without teacher credentials, Stossel argues that if this is not expressly outlawed in the Constitution, homeschooling without the need for credentials should be permitted.

As you read, consider the following questions:

1. As stated in the article, in 2006, what was the average ACT score of a homeschooled student?

2. In 2003, how many children nationwide were being homeschooled?

3. What argument does Stossel give for parents being constitutionally able to educate their children?

The cat is finally out of the bag. A California appellate court, ruling that parents have no constitutional right to homeschool their children, pinned its decision on this ominous quotation from a 47-year-old case, "A primary purpose of the educational system is to train schoolchildren in good citizenship, patriotism and loyalty to the state and the nation as a means of protecting the public welfare." There you have it; a primary purpose of government schools is to train schoolchildren "in loyalty to the state." Somehow that protects "the public welfare" more than allowing parents to homeschool their children, even though homeschooled kids routinely outperform government-schooled kids academically. In 2006, homeschooled students had an average ACT [a college admissions examination] composite score of 22.4. The national average was 21.1.

Justice H. Walter Croskey said, "California courts have held that under provisions in the Education Code, parents do not have a constitutional right to homeschool their children."

If that is the law in California, then Charles Dickens's Mr. Bumble is right: "the law is a ass, a idiot."

The Education Code

The California Constitution says, "A general diffusion of knowledge and intelligence being essential to the preservation of the rights and liberties of the people, the Legislature shall encourage by all suitable means the promotion of intellectual, scientific, moral, and agricultural improvement."

That doesn't appear to rule out homeschooling, unless you read it as a grant of absolute power to politicians.

Admittedly, the education code is vague. It requires children to attend public school or a private school, where certified teachers are not required. But they can also be taught by state-credentialed tutors. Homeschooling is not directly addressed. There's disagreement over what that means. The court and the teachers' union claim homeschooling is illegal unless the teaching parent has state credentials.

Homeschooling parents, many of whom have declared their homes private schools, say what they do is legal. Up till now that's been fine with the California Department of Education. And California reportedly has 166,000 homeschoolers.

Nationwide, the National Center for Education Statistics says that in 2003 (the latest year for which it has a number), almost 1.1 million children were being homeschooled. The numbers keep increasing, so clearly homeschooling parents think their kids get something better at home than they would from public schools.

Why Do Parents Need Credentials While Private School Teachers Don't?

The *Los Angeles Times* isn't sure where the state law stands. "If no such right [to homeschool] exists, as a court ruled, the Legislature should make it an option," the newspaper's editorial board said. The editorial wondered why parents who teach one or two children at home need credentials, while private school teachers in classes full of kids don't.

The danger in having the legislature clarify the law is that the legislature is controlled by politicians sympathetic to the teachers' union, which despises homeschooling. "[H]ome-schoolers fear that any attempt to protect home-schooling would end up outlawing it," *Orange County Register* columnist Steven Greenhut writes.

It reminds me of what New York Judge Gideon Tucker said in the 19th century, "No man's life, liberty, or property are safe while the legislature is in session." This particular case is muddied by suspicions of child abuse, but as the *Times* said, the court improperly "used a single example of possible child abuse to throw the book at tens of thousands of home schoolers."

I think the state court is looking at the state Constitution upside down. The court finds no constitutional right to homeschool one's children. But in a free country, people are free to do anything not expressly prohibited by law. If the Constitution is silent about homeschooling, then the right is reserved to the people. That's how the framers of the American Constitution said things are supposed to work.

Re-evaluate Homeschooling

Last week [April 2008], the appellate court surprised everyone by agreeing to rehear the case. The *San Francisco Chronicle* reports that the judges "hinted at a re-evaluation of its entire Feb. 28 ruling by inviting written arguments from state and local education officials and teachers' unions."

On top of that, state schools' Superintendent Jack O'Connell says he thinks homeschooling is legal and favors choice in education.

That's reasonable news. But why is education the business of government? It's taken for granted that the state is every child's ultimate parent, but there's no justification for that in a free society. Parents may not be perfect—some are pretty bad—but a cold, faceless bureaucracy is no better.

Let's hope the court gets it right in June.

Periodical Bibliography

The following articles have been selected to supplement the diverse views presented in this chapter.

Sun Kyu Bae "Why Some States Require Teacher Certification for Homeschool," ProntoLessons, June 19, 2009. www.prontolessons.com.

Denis Cummings "How Should Government Regulate Homeschooling?" FindingDulcinea: Librarian of the Internet, September 17, 2009. www.findingdulcinea.com.

Billy Greer "Common Sense Regulation," *F.U.N. News* (Family Unschoolers Network), no. 12, December 11, 2006. www.unschooling.org.

Home School Legal Defense Association "Homeschool Non-Discrimination Bill Introduced in Congress," September 14, 2005. http://nche.hslda.org.

Jay Mathews "Three Smart Rules for Home School Regulation," Class Struggle Blog, August 21, 2009. http://voices.washingtonpost.com/class-struggle.

Andrea Natekar "Home-schooling Parents Worry About Certification," *East Valley Tribune*, March 16, 2008. www.eastvalleytribune.com.

Jessica Parnell "Homeschooling and Certification," Homeschooling Help Blog, August 23, 2009. http://jessica-parnell.com.

Brian D. Ray and Bruce K. Eagleson "State Regulation of Homeschooling and Homeschoolers' SAT Scores," *Academic Leadership*, vol. 6, no. 3, August 14, 2009. www.academicleadership.org.

Susan Ryan "Review—'Write These Laws on Your Children,'" *Home Education Magazine*, August 2009. www.homedmag.com.

CHAPTER 3

Who Should Homeschool?

Chapter Preface

Teen mothers have to both care for their children and attend school. Balancing these demands can be difficult. One solution that teen mothers sometimes try is homeschooling.

Milton Gaither, a professor at Messiah College, wrote about homeschool for teen mothers in a July 22, 2008, post on his blog Homeschooling Research Notes, looking in particular at a study of teen mothers undertaken by researcher Lee Smith-Battle. According to Gaither, SmithBattle found that teen mothers often became more determined to succeed after they became pregnant. Thus, according to Gaither, "parenthood often fosters a sense of maturity and responsibility." Nonetheless, the teen mothers often come from poor and disadvantaged backgrounds, so success remains very difficult.

One of the major problems the teen mothers in the study faced was scheduling—getting to school, caring for their children, and often working on the side were extremely challenging. Gaither reported that SmithBattle's research found that "girls whose school districts provided at-home tutoring had a much easier time making it work. . . . Students who received at-home tutoring . . . were able to do schoolwork between feedings without the social challenges endemic to low-grade high schools." On the other hand, where schools refused to provide at-home tutoring, the teen mothers had a much more difficult time. Schools in urban areas, SmithBattle reported, were especially unwilling to provide home tutoring. Gaither says that SmithBattle "relates several heartbreaking stories of earnest efforts by these young women to continue their educations that are rebuffed by inflexible school bureaucracies."

Though homeschooling can help teen mothers in some instances, it is not a cure-all. For instance, an article by Darryl Campagna for Women's eNews on May 13, 2001, discusses some of the limitations of homeschooling for teen mothers. One profiled girl, Iris Colondres, had problems during her pregnancy and was forced to receive tutoring at home, but "the home tutor showed up so irregularly" that Colondres failed several courses and had to take her junior year over.

Homeschooling can also be used as a means to keep teens with children out of sight. Pregnant teens are sometimes seen as an embarrassment to the school. Homeschooling can be a way to get teen mothers and pregnant teens out of sight, and teaching in such programs may be inadequate. Thus Susan Berke Fogel of the California Women's Law Center in Los Angeles, argues against forcing teen mothers into homeschooling. Fogel, Campagna noted, believed that "studying at home or leaving a regular high school should be an option, not an ultimatum." In the following viewpoints, authors evaluate the pros and cons of homeschooling for African Americans, autistic children, Christian families, and other groups.

> "Schools in general breed conformity . . . [to] norms that include . . . manifestations of media messages about beauty standards, consumerism, and gender roles that my feminist ideology fundamentally opposes."

Feminist Homeschooling Benefits Mothers and Children

Rachel Allen

Rachel Allen is a former public relations director for the California chapter of the National Organization for Women (NOW). In the following viewpoint, she argues that the curriculums taught in schools perpetuate sexism, racism, and media ideas about gender, which, as a feminist, she politically opposes. By homeschooling, she says, she has been able to teach her child greater political awareness and a greater appreciation for diversity and learning.

As you read, consider the following questions:

1. According to Allen, one problem with media is that they put out negative messages about what?

Rachel Allen, "Feminist Parenting: Taking on the World, One Kid at a Time," California NOW, August 4, 2008. Reproduced by permission.

2. What has been Allen's family's experience with public schools?

3. What are some of the everyday, real-life activities in which Allen and her homeschooled children participate?

The onslaught of media consumed by children today cannot be avoided. Even if your kids don't consume it directly, their friends will. Negative messages about body image, overt and thinly veiled racism, sexism and homophobia are everywhere, and our children absorb all that in a variety of ways. In addition to trying to change the media—which must be a critical part of movements for social justice—as parents we have to act as mediators between the messages our children get in the world, and how those messages affect who they are and what they believe.

School Is Dangerous

Schools are places where media messages—the effects of them and children's interpretations of them—are mixed with real-life experiences with institutionalized bigotry and oppression. From the far corners of the playground where child anarchy can foster unchecked messages and experiences, to the history books that formalize those sentiments, too often our kids are being schooled in a context that, as feminists, we know is dangerous.

That's why, as a feminist mother, I chose to not send my kids to school.

In addition to being a feminist parent, I am a feminist homeschooler. This has been a difficult identity to reconcile within me. I have always been a strong believer in the public school system. I am 100% a product of it. My parents are teachers. My husband taught for seven years. My daughter went to one year of school, enjoyed it and had no terrible experience that made me yank her out and run away. I understand the belief that public education is a cornerstone of our democracy. I know a lot of teachers who work really hard to have democratic classrooms, teach tolerance and address social issues. But, I can't get past the fact that schools in general breed conformity, conformity to norms that include sexist, racist, classist, heterosexist and homophobic underpinnings; norms that include manifestations of media messages about beauty standards, consumerism, and gender roles that my feminist ideology fundamentally opposes. And although I know I can't shield my kids from all of that, I can minimize the influence without living in a bubble and provide an education that implicitly opposes those things.

Homeschooling Allows More Freedom

Part of what homeschooling affords us is the opportunity to be out in our community participating in our democracy, studying it and critiquing it. In a traditional classroom, students too often are subjects of totalitarianism, not a democracy. They may study government, but it is only in the abstract, and much of the teachings include blatant lies about its formation and intentions. We are able to focus on the peoples' history and learn to be better citizens of the world.

As parents, we are on hand to address misconceptions and to take on negative media and the big issues affecting the world. Most of all, we encourage critical thinking. Not just in the abstract, but of what our children hear and read and consume through media on a daily basis. They are now quick to discern what the motivation of corporations are, how advertising works, and what ideas are embedded in what they encounter. My daughter especially is quick to point out that her books on babysitting are always geared towards girls, and that toys and books aimed at girls are too often focused on superficial things like fashion.

Because of the freedom of our schedule, we do not confine the study of women to March [Women's History Month] or African Americans to February [Black History Month].

A Quandary for Feminist Moms

Even though the [do-it-yourself] approach may appeal to progressives who identify with the antiestablishment ethos of the punk movement, homeschooling still raises tricky questions for progressive mothers.

Namely, this one: Can women trade their careers for their families without sacrificing a few of their feminist values—the very values that inspired many of them to homeschool in the first place? It's no wonder that punk feminist moms like Kim Campbell, who has home-schooled her kids for seven years, occasionally feel like walking oxymorons. . . .

Campbell worries that her economic dependence on her husband could set a bad example for her daughter. "The first half year . . . I knew that I was making a great decision, but I couldn't figure out how to square it with what I'd always considered my feminist sensibilities." For Campbell and a growing contingent of other feminist unschoolers across the country, educating their kids has also been a process of figuring out how homeschooling jibes with their feminism.

Maya Schenwar, "Learning Curve,"
Bitch Magazine, 2008. http://bitchmagazine.org.

When art exhibits and antiwar marches and special speakers on campus come up, we can go. When something sparks their interest, my kids can follow that interest through without being too busy doing inane worksheets for homework, and don't have to study only what the state has decided a child in that grade should be studying. My children are out in the world, observing some women and people of color in high-powered positions, and some living in poverty. They observe homophobia, sexism, racism and classism in the world, and we are right there to help them identify and process, and even work to address those injustices.

Homeschoolers See the Real World

Because I work from home, as an activist in the women's movement, my children also see what it looks like to work for change. They see me, and other women, working in a variety of jobs, instead of believing the children's books that feature women always as teachers, nurses or ballerinas. When they are with us throughout our day, they also see up close how to live a socially conscious life. They see that we shop locally, honor labor, and boycott stores like Wal-Mart [Wal-Mart has been accused of violating employees' rights]. They learn how to communicate with adults, work on their relationships with friends and family, and be conscious of the decisions they make and how they affect others. They go with us to vote and to attend organizing meetings. These are the real-life lessons, and illustrations of the personal as political, that I believe are cornerstones of their education and of their personal development.

In their interactions with other children, of which there are many (and if my daughter had a choice they would be constant), the grown-ups are able to help our children practice being peacemakers, being inclusive and compassionate friends and citizens of a community. The group of families we homeschool with have exposed my children to ideas and art and lifestyles that are varied and different from our own, and that difference is celebrated. The children are able to take on service learning projects in our community, volunteer their time to charitable endeavors and raise money to help those in need.

Homeschooling for us is a way to provide an education that is implicitly justice focused, that takes on—instead of ingrains—the dangerous aspects of our government and society.

This framework allows them to think critically and act accordingly. It hopefully inspires them to think outside the boxes children (and adults) are pushed into, and to take on the injustices in their world. As a feminist mother, this is way more in line with the kind of parent I want to be, and the kind of kids I want to raise.

| "Homeschooling as a solution that's feminist for the children is much harder to defend on feminist terms for the parent."

Feminist Homeschooling Is Problematic

Patricia R. Stokes

Patricia R. Stokes (Sungold) is a blogger who writes mostly about feminism and parenthood. In the following viewpoint, she argues that, in practice, feminism and homeschooling are hard to reconcile because homeschooling requires one parent, usually the mother, to stay home. As a result, the mother is economically dependent and vulnerable in case of divorce or death of the husband. Thus, from a feminist perspective, homeschooling is often not good for the mother, even if it has advantages in some situations for children.

As you read, consider the following questions:

1. When the author wrote this viewpoint, how many children did she have, and into what years of school were they rising?

Patricia R. Stokes, writing as Sungold, "Feminist Homeschooling: Why I Don't," Kitty wampus.wordpress.com. From Kittywampus.blogspot.com, August 6, 2008. Reproduced by permission of the author.

2. According to the viewpoint, some stay-at-home mothers may decide to stay home with the assumption that what won't strike them personally?

3. Under what conditions does the author say that homeschooling might be the least-bad choice for her family?

The core of [Rachel Allen's] argument [in her 2008 article "Feminist Parenting: Taking on the World, One Kid at a Time"] is that schools are basically racist, sexist, homophobic engines of conformity that magnify the most pernicious aspects of the mass media. Homeschooling offers her a way to counteract those forces while maintaining a work-at-home career as a feminist activist.

Homeschooling and Work

In principle, I think homeschooling can be made compatible with any worldview. In my little town, as in most of America by now, the homeschool community is composed partly of fundamentalist or conservative Christians, partly of lefty/ alternative/neo-hippie families. I also know people with non-ideological reasons for homeschooling: They have gifted or speech-delayed kids who are served poorly by their local school, or they faced a bullying problem that couldn't be resolved.

In practice, however, I think feminist homeschooling is a thorny issue, if only because it requires one parent to be mostly at home. Rachel Allen is lucky in that she works from home. I know another political activist in my neighborhood who strikes a similar balance. Most of us don't have that much flexibility.

As a university professor I have more flexibility than most workers, but I couldn't homeschool unless I had a nanny to carry much of the burden. I still have to show up for my classes and meetings. This year, I've got a rising third grader

The Mommy Tax

When you've been home raising children, you are looked at (by employers) as if your brain has been on ice, so you take a hit in your income. . . . I put a name on it: The Mommy Tax. In other words, what is your lifetime loss of income if you have a kid, in terms of lowered income for the rest of your life? . . . If a college-educated woman has one child, she will lose about a million dollars in lifetime earnings. I didn't have my child until I was over 40, and I already had a number of years working. But my Mommy Tax is close to a million.

Ann Crittenden, as told to Katy Abel,
"The Price of Motherhood: An Interview with Ann Crittenden,"
FamilyEducation.com. www.familyeducation.com.

and kindergartner. With both kids in public school, I'm looking forward to going full-time (and having my own health insurance!) after nearly a decade of part-time work.

For work reasons alone, then, I wouldn't homeschool unless I felt there was no other tenable solution. Of course, I realize that I'm lucky to have work that's personally rewarding and reasonably remunerative.

The Risks for Mom

And this points to the crux of the problem of reconciling feminism with homeschooling: While the kids may be getting an anti-sexist, anti-racist, anti-homophobic education, the stay-at-home parent is still usually a mother. If she works from home for pay, she rarely earns enough to survive financially if her marriage or partnership were to end. So homeschooling as a solution that's feminist for the children is much harder to defend on feminist terms for the parent.

I don't think that staying home to parent is inherently anti-feminist. I did it myself when my kids were little, and it's important, honorable work. It's just that the longer you stay out of the labor market, the more precarious your financial position will be—and if that situation persists for a couple of decades, the stay-at-home parent is likely to be very vulnerable, financially. Sure, there are ways to mitigate this by working part-time or from home, or by taking turns being the at-home parent. But the fact remains that as Ann Crittenden[1] has shown so persuasively, staying at home has very steep, long-term costs.

I'm the last person to measure worth and happiness solely in financial terms (otherwise I wouldn't have spent all that time in grad school). However, I see lots of female students hoping to be stay-at-home parents without much awareness of the attendant risk of poverty, and I suspect many mothers decide to stay home with the assumption that divorce or widowhood won't strike them personally.

The calculation changes, of course, if you live somewhere with poor schools. We're lucky in that our local elementary school is quite good. The teachers are smart, dedicated, and fairly progressive. Though I live in predominantly white Appalachia, the student body is multiethnic and multinational, partly because the school serves the university's graduate student population, partly because binational families like mine gravitate toward its diversity.

Diversity is of course no safeguard against racism, sexism, or homophobia. I know of at least one incident where a racist joke was told at recess. Lunchtime conversation too often revolves around gender stereotypes. The teachers can't police all of this, and so it's up to us parents to talk to our kids after school and discuss why those things aren't okay.

1. Ann Crittenden's book *The Price of Motherhood: Why the Most Important Job in the World Is Still the Least Valued* argued that in America women who choose to stay at home suffer economically.

School Provides Diversity and Stimulation

Homeschooling would shield my kids from hateful and ste-reotypical comments. On the flip side, though, they wouldn't learn how to respond to racism and sexism, which my rising third grader already does pretty effectively. The school envi-ronment is also much more diverse than our local home-schooling community in terms of race, nationality, social class, and parents' educational level.

I fully agree with Rachel Allen that there's pressure to con-form even in [the] most progressive schools. One of our jobs as parents, I think, is to help kids learn to distinguish between mindless conformity and the necessity to get along and work well with others. So far, we're all doing okay, but I'm well aware that striking this balance won't get easier over time.

Temperamentally, homeschooling would be a tough fit for my kids. My older son, the Bear, wouldn't *want* homeschool-ing; we've talked about it, and we both know it would turn into a contest of wills, me nagging, him resisting. He also needs more stimulation than any one parent could provide, and he gets that primarily from the other kids at school, plus frequent playdates and oodles of informal teaching after school. The Bear's curiosity never sleeps. (For that matter, the Bear would literally prefer never to sleep, and he's been that way since the day he was born.) Even with all the activities that homeschooling families pursue together, we'd still come up short.

I can imagine certain circumstances where homeschooling might be the least-bad choice for us: if one of my boys was getting severely bullied and was unable to learn; if he was so terminally bored that his grades were suffering (their dad dropped out of school, actually, for that reason); or if we moved somewhere that had lousy schools. But for now, I'm grateful that my kids are in good hands at their school. We've been lucky to have good, close relationships with their teachers. I'm eager to finally put more energy into my own work (feminist and otherwise) after nearly a decade of dialing back those commitments.

Not least, the kids get along better when they're not together 24/7, and for that reason alone, we're counting down to August 26 [the start of the school year].

"A Godless curriculum will produce a Godless people."

Christians Have a Responsibility to Homeschool

Dan Smithwick

Dan Smithwick is the founder of the Nehemiah Institute, a non-profit foundation that creates and distributes Christian educational materials. In the following viewpoint, he argues that the corruption of modern society is mostly owing to the spread of secular, state-run education. Education without God, Smithwick maintains, is both sinful and incomplete. He concludes that Christians have a responsibility to their children and to God to stay away from the secular education found in public schools.

As you read, consider the following questions:

1. Who was John Taylor Gatto, and what did he warn against?

2. According to Smithwick, why is an unsafe environment last on the list of top nine reasons for Christians not to use the public schools?

3. Smithwick claims that the United States was founded as what kind of nation?

Dan Smithwick, "Nine Reasons for Not Using Public Schools," *Home School Digest*, July 19, 2004. Copyright © 2005 Wisdom's Gate. Reproduced by permission

Public schools (or as some like to say, government schools) have come upon hard times in the past several years. One would be hard-pressed to find a community where the public school system is not having serious problems. While gun shootings get the most coverage, understandably, there are many, many other problems plaguing the 150-year-old experiment of government-run education. Budget crises, teacher shortages, facility problems, undisciplined youth, and now more frequently, problem parents plague most school districts. In addition to these is the fundamental problem—poor education. Standardized test scores have fallen dramatically over the past few decades. Both college and business leaders lament how poorly high school students are educated.

For the first two centuries of our nation, civil government had no role in education. In the last century, it has wanted to be the only role. We spend more money on education per pupil than any other industrialized nation yet we rank near or at the bottom in academic performance, especially in math, physics and sciences. Why? The answer is theological in every sense.

I want to give nine reasons why the church today should cease using state-run schools. I also want to acknowledge up front that there are oftentimes circumstances why Christians believe they have to use the public schools. It is neither my place, nor anyone else's I believe, to judge all situations from afar. I will say more on this later. First, some background on the theological basis for arguing why the church should abandon government schooling.

Schools Have Abandoned God

Here is the fundamental issue:

Jesus said, "Man shall not live by bread alone, but by every Word that proceeds from the mouth of God" (Matthew 4:4). For the past several decades it appears that leaders of our nation, particularly in the field of education, have systematically set out to demonstrate that Jesus didn't know what He was talking about. From the removal of the Ten Commandments in the classroom to denying prayer in school to forbidding any display of religious objects in public places (including a closed Bible on a teacher's desk), our nation has determined to become a secular people officially. No Word, just bread; no supernatural, just natural.

The fruit of this removal of Christianity from the public square is apparent to anyone who wants to see—a decrease in good things (honesty, morality, literacy, family coherence, etc.) and an increase in bad things (crime, sexual immorality, bankruptcies, business and government corruption, family breakdown, etc.). Within a few short generations, our nation has been changing from liberty to bondage (government dependency), from free enterprise to socialism, from creditor status to debtor status, from community spirit to isolationism, from honoring God to ignoring Him.

The seedbed for this change, I believe, more than any other place, has been the public school classroom. When the public/government school system began in the early 19th century, it was absorbed in an environment of Christian ethics held to publicly and privately since the days of the Pilgrims. Bible reading and fear of the Lord were the foundations of learning. Not anymore. The spiritual capital inherited by the public school system has been spent and will not be replenished.

But America didn't enter this experiment of nonreligious secular education without warning. Theologian and educator Dr. A.A. Hodge, Princeton Theological Seminary said, "I am sure as I am of Christ's reign that a comprehensive and centralized system of national education, separated from religion, as is now commonly proposed, will prove the most appalling enginery for the propagation of anti-Christian and atheistic unbelief, and of antisocial nihilistic ethics, individual, social and political, which this sin-rent world has ever seen."

Scholar J. Gresham Machen said, "An education that trains the mind without training the moral sense is a menace to civilization rather than a help." On January 12, 1926, Machen testified before a congressional committee on the dangers of creating a federal Department of Education. He stated, "Do we want a federal Department of Education, or do we not? I think we do not, and I am asking your permission to tell you very briefly why. We do not, I think, want a federal Department of Education because such a Department is in the interests of a principle of uniformity or standardization in education which would be the very worst calamity into which this country could fall."

Martin Luther said, "I'm afraid that the schools will prove the very gates of hell, unless they diligently labor in explaining the Holy Scriptures and engraving them in the heart of youth." America's government-run education system has proven Luther right.

These men, and many others, gave us clear warnings about government-run, secular, no-Bible education, but churches pressed on. They bought the concept of "free" education and surrendered their posterity to be raised by the state. Would to God that all parents would have seen the error of this as early as one parent from Iowa who said, "I don't want my children fed by the state. I don't want my children clothed by the state, but I would prefer either to their being educated by the state."

"Insider" John Taylor Gatto, 1991 New York State Teacher of the Year, speaker, author of *Dumbing Us Down: The Hidden Curriculum of Compulsory Schooling* and *The Exhausted School: Bending the Bars of Traditional Education*, stated, "We live in a time of great school crises. Our children rank at the bottom of nineteen industrial nations in reading, writing and arithmetic. At the very bottom. Our teenage suicide rate is the highest in the world, and suicidal kids are rich kids for the most part, not the poor. In Manhattan fifty percent of all new marriages last less than five years. Something is wrong for sure."

Education expert Samuel L. Blumenfeld stated, "The plain, unvarnished truth is that public education is a shoddy, fraudulent piece of goods sold to the public at an astronomical price. It's time the American consumer knew the extent of the fraud which is victimizing millions of children each year."

Pastor and author Douglas Wilson captured the situation well by saying in *Recovering the Lost Tools of Learning: An Approach to Distinctively Christian Education* (1991), "For over one hundred years, Americans have been running a gigantic experiment in government schools, trying to find out what a society looks like without God. Now we know."

Here are my nine reasons why Christians should no longer use public schools (and really never should have)—listed in reverse order.

Unsafe Environment

Surely, every parent in America has heard about the gun shootings in more than a dozen public schools over the past several years. What mom hasn't worried as she watched her children go off to school wondering if today it might happen to them? But there are tens of thousands of students who go to their public school daily without ever being confronted with such violence. There are lesser-degree acts of violence (fights, sexual abuse, name calling, teasing, etc.), but these problems show up in private schools as well. Even drug and alcohol problems occur in Christian schools. Public schools are unsafe in many ways, but I believe it belongs last on the list of "top nine" reasons for Christians not enrolling their children in them.

Negative Role Models

The Bible says, "Do not be deceived: bad company corrupts good morals" (1 Cor. 15:33). An environment where the majority of people are not Christian is unquestionably going to produce a different ethic than will occur when nearly all are Christian (faculty and students). The value system, or worldview, of non-Christian teachers and students will produce a "normal" environment that is hostile to Christianity. If we believe the Bible to be true, it simply cannot be any different.

Most students like to model their teachers, especially when they are viewed as "cool." However, the morals of Christian-family youth are being corrupted when the lifestyle of their teachers reflects such anti-Christian views as gay "rights," abortion "rights" and sex before marriage. Believing otherwise is already proof that the warning of this Scripture was ignored—you have been deceived.

Reverse Evangelism

Many Christian families state that a key reason for staying with the public school system is to be "salt and light" to a pagan culture. I think this may be an excellent reason for an adult who is called to teach and who has a burden for evangelism of the lost. There are many Christian teachers in public schools who choose their work for this reason, and my hat goes off to them. They are undoubtedly facing in-your-face hostility to Christian principles yet remain there to pray for the lost, be a witness for Christ, and give the best education they can to students, but the "salt and light" concept ends there. I think it is unwise (dangerous) to send little-trained or untrained youth to perhaps the key battleground of humanists (the public school classroom) and expect them to be effective in winning over unbelievers—adult or student. The evangelism is working in reverse far too often as is evidenced by Christian-family youth adopting morals of their unbelieving friends.

Godless Curriculum

School is about learning, and learning is about knowing truth. Fundamental to Christian faith is the axiom that God *IS* truth. God chose to reveal Himself in Word-form (the outworking of truth) in four primary ways: 1) by His spoken Word—"Let there be . . ." Creation came into existence with order and purpose; 2) by inspiration—His written Word was given to us in the Scriptures for right living; 3) by incarnation—His Word was given to us in flesh (Jesus Christ) for our redemption; and 4) by His final Word all will be judged, "For all who have sinned without the Law will also perish without the Law, and all who have sinned under the Law will be judged by the Law" (Romans 5:12).

When schools use curriculum that is completely void of God's Word, how can we possibly expect students to be educated? How can we expect our children to be blessed? To be successful? Peter Marshall [a Presbyterian minister and writer on America's Christian heritage] said, "Let us not fool ourselves—without Christianity, without Christian education, without the principles of Christ inculcated into young life, we are simply rearing pagans." A Godless curriculum will produce a Godless people.

Public Schooling Is Not Thorough

Pick any subject taught in K–12 education. If it has been taught apart from the knowledge revealed in Scripture, it is incomplete (and likely inaccurate). History, biology, mathematics, sociology, science, language, arts, economics, government—each are openly addressed in Scripture. In other words, the God who made all creation has also told us how to understand creation. Why would we want to go to the effort and expense of having our children educated for 12–16 years ignoring what the original Author has to say about the subjects we are teaching? It makes no sense, except for the fallen mind who wants no part of God. As Christians, we understand this dilemma for the unbeliever, but why should we give our children to them for the primary education of their lives?

Take history for example. Schools teach world history, but do students in government schools learn the factual history of mankind: formations of people groups, nations, or why certain civilizations came and went? Or, the origins of different languages? Do they learn of the individuals who were greatly used of God in shaping civilization—Noah? Abraham? Moses? David? Paul? Are they taught about some of the world's greatest events such as creation, the flood, the birth, death and resurrection of the Son of God (by whom the school's calendar is dated)? Not likely.

What about U.S. history? It is beyond the scope of this [viewpoint] to make the case for America's foundation being squarely laid upon Christianity. I will only quote [evangelical minister] Dr. D. James Kennedy, "Today there are those who gnash their teeth at the very mention of the fact that America was founded as a Christian nation, but the facts of history are not easily dismissed, though they are certainly ignored in our schools and in many of our modern, revisionist history books." Yet, public schools have dismissed this part of U.S. history. Students can receive an "A" in history and never have to know what the original Author had to say or to know of His hand on our history. This is not education.

Poor Academic Results

It is secret to none: Public school students, to a large degree, are simply not well-educated. Much has been written about the "dumbing down" of our public schools. There are exceptions of course. Some youth, because of their gifting and good homes, are excelling in public schools in spite of the overall deterioration of the system, but for the great majority, even average to above average in intelligence, they are being badly educated. What a travesty this is.

My friend, Rev. E. Ray Moore, Jr., recently wrote, "Abundant evidence, assembled from test scores and elsewhere, assures us that today's public school graduates do not have the mastery of basic subjects that earlier generations had. Students are leaving public high schools in record numbers without having acquired basic writing skills, reading comprehen-

---

Reasons for Homeschooling, 2003

Percentages do not sum to 100% because respondents could choose more than one reason.

Reasons for homeschooling	Applicable Percent	Most Important Percent
Concern about environment of other schools	85.4	31.2
Dissatisfaction with academic instruction at other schools	68.2	16.5
To provide religious or moral instruction	72.3	29.8
Child has a physical or mental health problem	15.9	6.5
Child has other special needs	28.9	7.2
Other reasons	20.1	8.8

TAKEN FROM: National Center For Education Statistics, "Table 4: Number and Percentage of Homeschool Students..." *Homeschooling in the United States: 2003*, February 2006. http://nces.ed.gov.

---

sion, or mathematical ability. They know little or nothing of this country's founding or its history. They cannot place major historical figures or events in the right century. They cannot walk up to wall maps and point out significant foreign countries. This intellectual deterioration has spread into public colleges and universities that have admitted more and more unprepared students into college-level work."

Government Schooling Breeds the View That Success Can Be Obtained Apart from God

If we throw out all the bad stuff found in public schools (shootings, rapes, stealing, fighting, cheating, etc.) and have a "nice" school where no student is afraid, we are still left with an education system that is robbing youth of the most important aspect of being educated—to trust God. The supreme value being touted today for education is so you can be successful and have a good life. Students are told, "You need a good education so you can get a good job so you can give your children a good education so they can get a good job," ad infinitum [to infinity]. Not only is this a horrible philosophy of life, it is grossly un-biblical. The Bible says, "But you shall remember the LORD your God, for it is He who is giving you power to make wealth" (Deuteronomy 8:18), but this wealth is not simply for the sake of our being rich, for this verse continues, "that He may establish His covenant which He swore to your fathers, as it is this day."

Here is the purpose of being properly educated and successful—to establish God's covenant on earth. Government schools do not go this direction but rather promote materialism as a way of being successful. This is a formula for failure, the exact opposite of the stated purpose of public education.

Government Schooling Produces No Fear of God

Now we are getting closer to the heart of the problem with secular, government-run education. God said, "Remember the day you stood before the LORD your God at Horeb, when the LORD said to me, 'Assemble the people to Me, that I may let them hear My words so they may learn to fear Me all the days they live on the earth, and that they may teach their children'" (Deuteronomy 4:10).

Fear of God is almost a lost concept in our culture. The meaning of the word fear as used in the above Scripture is: 1) morally to revere; and 2) causatively to frighten. Five times in the Book of Deuteronomy the phrase "learn and fear" is found in the context of knowing God's Word. The reason there is little shame anymore (have you seen any lately?) is because there is no fear of God anymore.

Horace Mann and John Dewey, founders of our public school system, openly expressed their hatred for Christianity. They literally feared an education system that would teach youth to fear God, which is just what America had for the first two hundred years of existence. Jesus had a very different view about fear: "Do not fear those who kill the body but are unable to kill the soul; but rather fear Him who is able to destroy both soul and body in hell" (Matthew 10:28). It would now be considered illegal to quote this statement of Jesus in public schools.

Education, in any subject, should create fear (reverence) of God for how His majesty is revealed in that area of life. Teaching should also instill a proper fear (fright) of going against God's order and purpose in each discipline of life. Sadly, our public schools teach subjects simply as if God does not exist.

Public Schooling (Secular Education) Is Disobedience to God

Herein lies the primary reason why Christians should not use government schools. Having been educated myself in public school through college, having become a Christian at age 33, and having put our five children through combinations of public and private Christian schools, I can only look back and confess that I was not always obedient in "education." I wish every day I could relive some of those years and do it "by the Book," but those days are gone. It is only the present in which we can decide to be obedient in this all-important field we call education.

The Bible says, "Train up a child in the way he should go, even when he is old he will not depart from it" (Proverbs 22:6). There is simply no easy way around the fact that putting our children in an anti-Christian education system is not training them up in the way they should go. Many parents want to say, "But we are giving our children Bible training at home." Really? Are you going back to all the subject matter your children are taking and giving them a Scripture-based education to correct wrong teaching? If so, you are in essence homeschooling them, so why continue to have them enrolled in the government school? If you mean that you are giving your children moral training, and letting the government school give them "academic" training, you are simply denying them a Christian worldview. Your children are being given an anti-Christian worldview in all subjects at the local government school.

At the beginning of this [viewpoint] I acknowledged that there are Christians who sincerely believe that, for their situation, government schooling is what they need to use. In response, I would say that if you have sought pastoral counsel, prayed, and are trusting Christ for this decision and have peace that you are doing the right thing for your children, then walk in it. If you have not done these things, but are simply "doing what everybody else in church is doing," then I would like to challenge you to seek the Lord and get His mind on the matter of public schooling for your children.

"*I find it difficult and painful to imagine a public school system devoid of Christians. . . . Christians will have removed the best indigenous missionaries from their natural mission field.*"

Christians Have a Responsibility Not to Homeschool

Tim Challies

Tim Challies is a Canadian Web designer, blogger, and reviewer and the author of The Discipline of Spiritual Discernment. *In the following viewpoint, he explains that as a Christian he sends his children to public school for two main reasons. First, he believes that Christians are called to bring the Gospel to nonbelievers, and he thinks his children will best learn how to fulfill this mission by going to public school. Second, he feels that it is best for children to encounter the world early, when they look to parents for guidance, rather than encounter it later, when they are more likely to be misled.*

As you read, consider the following questions:

1. According to Challies, what about Christian schools makes them impractical for his family?

2. According to Challies, why are even young children equipped to be evangelists?

3. What examples does Challies give of teachings his children might encounter which run counter to the family's convictions?

For some time now I have been pondering the value of writing about the reasons that [my] wife and I have chosen to have our children educated through the public school system. Public schools are not the only option available to us. We are capable of homeschooling our children—we are both well-educated and each have a university degree. There are homeschooling groups in our town that we could tap into and endless numbers of homeschooling resources available to us. While it would definitely be a huge strain on our finances (to the point that either my wife or I might have to be willing to take on a part-time job), we could possibly even come up with $10,000 a year to enroll our children in a local Christian school. Practically, though, the options for my family come down to public schools or homeschool. We have chosen to place our children in public schools. And now I am going to tell you why.

Freedom of Conscience

Before I continue, I would like to affirm that I believe this is an area in which Christians have freedom from God to do what we feel is appropriate for our individual families.... I do not believe that any of the options—homeschooling, Christian schooling or public schooling—is inherently wrong, but feel that each family must follow their convictions on this matter. I do not judge or condemn those who choose other options. The real sin would be to violate one's conscience or to look negatively upon those who choose other options. . . .

Of course not everyone believes, as I do, that we have freedom in this area. To these people I urge charity. I grew up in a church where Christian schooling was expected and demanded. I have read any number of articles by those who choose to homeschool who believe that homeschooling is the only biblical option for educating children. While these people may make some valid arguments, I am not convicted by Scripture or by plain reason that we must avoid public schools.

There is one more thing I would like to say before I get too much further into this [viewpoint]. Homeschooling parents are easily offended (See? I offended you just by saying that!). Some may consider this a rash generalization, but in my experience it is true. Homeschoolers are often on the defensive, though certainly this is changing as homeschooling becomes a more widely accepted option in the church and in the wider culture. For many years homeschoolers have had to defend their choice in education and they have grown weary of defending against misunderstandings and straw man arguments. I am not going to argue that, if we homeschool, our children will end up having no social skills, we will have to move to the country to raise our own beef, I'll have to throw away my deodorant and my wife will have to grow her hair past her waist and begin making all of our clothes. I hope not to fall into caricatures of homeschooling. Feel free to correct me if I do. There is much I admire about those who choose to homeschool. Honest. At the same time, please do not use caricatures to describe public schools as being always boring, filled with disinterested Wiccan teachers or serving as training grounds for automatons who are being trained only to work in factories.

And with this in mind I would like to explain why my wife and I have chosen to have our children attend public schools. Please note the word "chosen." Some people seem to feel that only in the *absence* of conviction do parents send their children to public schools. This is not the case with my wife. Aileen and I, having spent a great deal of time thinking and praying over the options available to us, send our children to public schools on the basis of conviction. . . .

And all this is to say that my beliefs about the world and the culture and the relationship of Christians to them is a large part of what motivates me to send my children to public schools. Just as ideology is what motivates some Christians to homeschool, ideology motivates me to have my children in the public school system. I am convicted that my children ought to be in public schools. . . .

For Missions

I believe that God has called every Christian to missions, whether we are born, live and die in our native culture or whether we choose to move halfway around the world and immerse ourselves in another culture. Every Christian is called to missions, for the Great Commission has not been rescinded and will not be until the Lord returns. We are all expected to fulfill this Commission to the best of our abilities. And this is a world in desperate need of the Gospel. We have lived in our neighborhood for six years now and have never once seen even one of our neighbors head to church. As far as we know, we are the only Christians in the area. Canada is a spiritual wasteland and my heart bleeds for the people in this neighborhood, in this community, and this nation. As Christians, my wife and I are indigenous missionaries. God has placed us in this culture, among these people, and He expects us to reach out to them and to let the Gospel go forth.

Trusting that my children will grow up to be believers, I am convicted that it is my duty as a parent, and as a Christian parent, to prepare my children to fulfill that calling in their lives. I believe they can best heed this call by being in the culture in which God has seen fit to place them. I want them to be with kids who are not Christians, to be friends with them and to love them, to learn what separates them from their friends, and to begin to understand how their convictions make them different from others. I want them to see and know and understand and believe in the superiority of Christianity to any other religion or way of life. I want them to see what the world has to offer and to see that it quickly loses its lustre.

I believe missions can and should happen everywhere. I find it difficult and painful to imagine a public school system devoid of Christians. Imagine, if you will, that every Christian pulls their children from the public schools. There will be no more Christian clubs in junior high schools; there will be no more prayer meetings or Bible studies at high schools; there will be no witnessing, no conversions. Christians will have removed the best indigenous missionaries from their natural mission field. I want my children to learn how to witness to their friends and want them to do it. Assuming my children are or will soon be young Christians, I do not want to deny them the ability and privilege of witnessing to others. New Christians are filled with joy and excitement and, while they may not know a lot yet, they are usually excited to share the Gospel with others. I want my children to do this and to see their school as a mission ground. I want them to experience the joy of sharing their faith and to grow in their ability to do this.

For Love

There is another side to this. We genuinely love the people around us and want to know them, both so we can relate to them as friends and so we can, with God's help, witness to them of His love and grace. Our children build bridges to the neighborhood. In sending our children to public school, we are building these bridges with our neighbors as our children are building friendships with their children. We are building friendships on the basis of our kids' friendships. This is not to say, of course, that we only relate to our neighbors because we hope to convert them. We relate to them because we genuinely love them, care for them, and seek to know them both for what they can offer us and what we can offer them. We seek to love our neighbors as ourselves. We have credibility as neighbors and as members of this community by having our children attend the same schools as the other children. This weekend we are having a neighborhood-wide event in our home and every family who has accepted our invitation is a family whose children go to school with our children.

Now some may argue that young children are unready to be evangelists and that it is unfair to expect them of this. Once again, both experience and Scripture prove this a false assumption. If our children are believers, they are filled with the same Holy Spirit as you and I. They are equipped to reach out to the most tenderhearted segment of the population.

My wife and I feel called to reach out to the people in our neighborhood and our community. We simply do not feel we could honor God in this way and be as effective in doing it if we kept our children home. We would lose credibility, we would lose friendships, and we would lose access to the hearts of both children and their parents. At the same time, we would be raising our children with the expectation that they witness to others, all the while keeping them from the most natural context for them to witness, to learn how to witness, and to understand those to whom they will need to witness. Our deeds would contradict our words.

To Avoid Worldliness

I have often spoken to Christian parents who feel that public schooling offers too many opportunities for their children to become worldly. Their defenses of homeschooling often discuss the world's problems and are then punctuated by comments like "This is why we homeschool!" Worldliness is clearly

Different Environments Work for Different Children

What's a Christian parent to do ... when it comes to School Choice? ...

Just like adults, children are all different and flourish best in different types of environments. ...

I saw home schoolers that became Godly men and women who were well-rounded and fully functioning in both religious and secular culture ... but also saw some unable to deal successfully in the "real" world.

I witnessed some children sent to Christian schools who today are empowered men and women of the Lord having a powerful impact in our society. ... However, I saw others openly rebelling against their "forced" training. ...

I observed children from strong Christian families attend public schools and truly serve as "Salt and Light" to those around them. ... In the same hallways, I saw young tender Christians tainted by the Godless philosophy of peers and educators. ...

Bottom line, there is not a right or wrong answer to the schooling choice issue.

Finn Laursen, "School Choice:
Homeschool? Christian School? Public School?"
Christian Educators Association International. www.ceai.org.

a serious offense in God's eyes. It is an offense so serious that worldly people have to be concerned about their salvation, for as the Bible tells us, "Do not love the world or the things in the world. If anyone loves the world, the love of the Father is not in him." Here is how [evangelical minister and writer] John MacArthur defines worldliness: "Worldliness is any preoccupation with or interest in the temporal system of life that places anything perishable before that which is eternal." [Pastor] Iain Murray says it is "the mind-set of the unregenerate." Those who love the world, and who put what is perishable before what is eternal, are those who do not know the love of the Father.

But we do not avoid worldliness by secluding ourselves from the world. The key to escaping worldliness is not to avoid the world, but to avoid *acting* like the world and *thinking* like the world. To do this we do not escape the world, but allow ourselves to apprehend the allure of the world so it might lose its glow. The world has a natural attraction to all of us who have sinful hearts. Something within us, some dark corner of our hearts, longs to return to the world, to the old man. But with the help of the Holy Spirit, we soon see that the world offers nothing but counterfeit joy and happiness that are opposed to God. To think that we can keep our children from being worldly by sheltering them from the world is false. Sooner or later children will want to see what the world has to offer. It is far better to let them see it when their hearts are tender, their confidence is in their parents, and their abilities are limited. Children who do not experience the world until they are old enough to be able [to] partake in all its so-called pleasures are children who fall away.

I believe it is easier for children to avoid worldliness when they are exposed to the world. This may sound strange, so allow me to explain. I want my children to see what the world has to offer before they are old enough to explore it on their own, without parental guidance. I want my children to see and experience families where God is not at the center. There are aspects to unbelieving families that may appeal, especially when the children are young, but as they grow and mature, I think they will see that what the world offers is so obviously detrimental to both individuals and families. They will learn the value of faithfulness when they see families fractured by infidelity. They will learn the value of mom following her biblical convictions and staying home to be a homemaker when they see families where mom and dad do not arrive home until well after dark leaving the children with no oversight, no guidance. They will see that what mom and dad are teaching them is true.

The fact is that worldliness comes from within. Worldliness is not something that is forced upon people or that is extrinsic to them. Worldliness is intrinsic and arises from a person's sinful nature. A person who never experiences the wider culture can still be worldly. A child who never darkens the door of a public school may be far more worldly than one who does so every day. A child who is homeschooled or who goes to a Christian school is, in my experience, no more likely to avoid worldliness or to grow up to be a committed follower of Christ than one who goes to public school. Visit a Christian college and see if the homeschooled kids or the kids who went to Christian schools act consistently better than those who attended public schools. Experience shows that you will not find a difference based primarily on the breakdown of how the children were educated. Keeping my children out of the world is not going to keep them from being worldly. And, in fact, by allowing them to see the cost of worldliness, the cost of disobedience to God, they will see worldliness for what it really is. They will see that God's promises of blessing to those who honor Him are as true as His promises of the curses that come to those who forsake Him.

I believe I can equip my children to love God and to avoid worldliness by placing them in public schools where they can see for themselves the cost of forsaking God.

Homeschooling Still an Option

I think it is important to note that, in any educational choice, work remains to be done. Homeschoolers have to be deliberate about building bridges to the community and neighborhood. They have to deliberately seek ways of inviting unbelieving children into their homes and finding ways into the homes of unbelieving families. They have to seek ways of building credibility with those who live around them, of building community with them and of finding ways for their children to learn to witness to others. With those of us who choose to send our children to public school, we must be deliberate about understanding what our children are learning, interpreting it for them, and ensuring that they have a Christian worldview that allows them to filter these things themselves. We must ensure that they understand their sin and see that it is only the Holy Spirit that makes them any different from the other children in the school. In either case, academic education is only the starting point for building a life that honors God and fulfills His commandments and commission. . . .

I would like to make clear that it is possible that in the future my wife and I will need to rethink our position. A time may come when the school system degenerates to a place where we simply cannot allow our children to be there. A time may come when it just makes sense for us to explore other options. Because I do not regard any of the options are intrinsically wrong, they are all open to us if necessity dictates that we follow a different course. We hope to continue to prayerfully reflect on the state of the system and to make wise decisions.

Christians Need Not Fear the World

There is one more thing worth considering. While homeschooling is an option currently available to Americans and Canadians and people in some other corners of the world, it has not always been this way and will not always be this way. Even today in many nations parents have no choice but to place their children in schools where the teachers seek to lead them away from Christ. Do these children fall away? Were the children of Christians in the Soviet Union swept away into atheism? This is simply not the case! God's grace was and is more than able to overcome all manner of unbiblical teaching. While this may not justify a decision, it does show that God is powerful and will not allow His children to fall out of His grasp.

I am not afraid of the world and what it may do to my children. There is nothing the world can offer that is greater or stronger than God's grace. I am sure that my children, at one time or another, will encounter teachings that run contrary to our convictions. They will learn about evolution and will hear that all religions are the same. I know that this is coming and am already working with them to know how to think about these things and to know how to respond. I am teaching them to respond to such teachings with love and respect for the teacher, but with disdain for teachings that go against Scripture. I am teaching this to them while they are young and while they trust me more than they trust others!

I am praying for this grace to be operative in the lives of my children and trusting that it will be so. I am trusting that God will draw my children to Himself and, in so doing, reorient their desires and affections so they see as He sees and value what He values. And as I do that, I am preparing them to know the culture, to be in but not of it—to reach out to a culture that is so desperately in need of missionaries who carry with them the Gospel message of Jesus's death and resurrection.

Periodical Bibliography

The following articles have been selected to supplement the diverse views presented in this chapter.

Tina Cruz	"Autism and Homeschooling: Why?" Autism Sucks Blog, February 26, 2009. www.autismsucksrocks.blogspot.com.
Examiner.com	"Parenting & Autism 101: What About Homeschooling an Autistic Child?" August 1, 2009. www.examiner.com.
Jennifer James	"Trends in African-American Home Schooling," Suite101.com, March 16, 2003. www.suite101.com.
Jo-Lynne	"What Happens if Christians Abandon the Public Schools?" Musings of a Housewife Blog, September 25, 2006. www.musingsofahousewife.com.
Wendy McElroy	"Can a Feminist Homeschool Her Child," *Freeman: Ideas on Liberty*, vol. 52, no. 2, February 2002. www.thefreemanonline.org.
E. Ray Moore Jr.	"Salt & Light, The Great Commission & Who's Responsible for Educating Your Children," Exodus Mandate, July 2004. www.exodusmandate.org.
Nancy Mullane	"African-American Homeschoolers on the Rise," *Weekend Edition Sunday* (NPR), September 16, 2007. www.npr.org.
Jesse Scaccia	"The Case Against Homeschooling," Teacher, Revised Blog, May 30, 2009. http://teacherrevised.org.
Maya Schenwar	"Learning Curve," *Bitch Magazine*, 2008. www.bitchmagazine.org.
Tammy Takahashi	"Feminist Homeschooling," Just Enough and Nothing More Blog, July 9, 2007. http://justenough.wordpress.com.

What Methods Should Homeschoolers Use?

Chapter Preface

The Charlotte Mason method is one of the more popular homeschooling approaches. Mason was a British educator who worked during the late nineteenth and early twentieth centuries. She was herself mostly educated at home.

The best-known part of the Charlotte Mason method is the use of "living books instead of dry, factual textbooks," according to an article on the Web site SimplyCharlotteMason .com. Where textbooks are written by groups of people to instruct, living books are usually written by one person because he or she is passionate about or interested in a subject. An August 7, 2008, post on the blog SpunkyHomeschool listed examples of living books such as Corrie Ten Boom's *Hiding Place*, Ann Voskamp and Tonia Peckover's *A Child's Geography* series, Molière's plays, and the Bible.

Another important principle of the Charlotte Mason method is the use of narration, according to SimplyCharlotte Mason.com. Mason believed that students learned best not when they provided short factual answers, but rather when they were asked to tell, write, or draw out longer narratives explaining what they had learned. Mason also believed that younger children should, in general, be taught in short fifteen- or twenty-minute lessons and that these lessons should be interspersed with physical activity.

Mason also advocated making nature study an important part of education. In her book *Home Education*, Mason said, "Let [children] once get touch (sic) with nature, and a habit is formed which will be a source of delight through . . . life." Mason recommended sending children out on nature walks to find objects to bring back to their mother or teacher, which the student and instructor could then discuss together. Mason also suggested that children should keep notebooks in which they record their observations and findings. In an article titled

"Nature Study" on the MacBeth's Opinion Blog, the writer noted, "Nature study becomes the basis for the study of all other sciences—geology, biology, chemistry, physics, and astronomy can all be observed in nature."

Some of Charlotte Mason's ideas have been criticized. For example, an article on the Let's Homeschool Web site notes that Mason's short lessons may be too restrictive and that her focus on nature study may not allow for instruction in science ideas that cannot be easily viewed in nature. The same writer also notes that the use of living books instead of textbooks may not work well in some technical subjects. Despite such limitations, however, Mason's method remains a source of inspiration and ideas (if not always a strict blueprint) for both Christian and secular homeschoolers. Mason's own books, such as *Towards a Philosophy of Education*, continue to be read. Other authors have also written to explain her ideas to a contemporary audience. One of these is Catherine Levison, who published *A Charlotte Mason Education* in 1999 and *More Charlotte Mason Education* in 2001. In the following viewpoints, authors look at the pros and cons of some other homeschooling methods.

> *"I like using the state tests as an assessment tool. . . . It comforts me to have empirical evidence that [my son] is doing at least as well as his public school peers."*

Standardized Tests Can Be Helpful for Homeschoolers

Sandra Foyt

Sandra Foyt is a homeschooling parent, an activist, and a writer. In the following viewpoint, she explains that, in the homeschool setting, standardized tests are much less stressful than in regular schools. Though they are not required in lower grades, she says, she has found them useful in assessing her child's strengths and weaknesses. Though she feels that standardized tests in school are usually not helpful, for her child at home they were useful and helped reassure her that her son was progressing normally.

As you read, consider the following questions:

1. In what grade will a homeschooled student in New York first be required to take a standardized test?

2. According to Foyt, which test was longer, the PASS test or the CAT-E test? Which did she prefer, and why?

Sandra Foyt, "Assessments and the Homeschooled Student," Onlivingbylearning.com, June 5, 2009. www.onlivingbylearning.com. Reproduced by permission of the author.

3. According to Foyt, why are standardized tests not helpful when administered to students in school?

Testing requirements and practice for homeschooled students differ by state and by family, much like they differ by state and teacher in the public schools.

Some homeschool families may satisfy their assessment requirements by doing absolutely nothing, while others may devote a significant part of their day to test prep and/or testing itself.

I'd say we're in the middle.

New York Homeschool Assessment Requirements

In grades 1–3, homeschooled New Yorkers are not required to take an assessment test. They can satisfy state requirements with a written narrative that:

1. Uses the regulation's required phrase: "[Child] has made adequate academic progress this year."

2. Lists two or three "highlights of the year," as insurance against claims that the "narrative" isn't really a narrative.

3. Ends with, "See the previously submitted quarterly reports for details." (Thank you, John Munson, NYHEN [New York Home Educators' Network]—Support Yahoo Forum.)

This narrative is to be written by a "certified teacher, peer review panel, or other person, who has interviewed the child and reviewed a portfolio of the child's work . . . [and who] shall be chosen by the parent with the consent of the superintendent." Parents can also prepare this narrative, with prior approval of the superintendent.

Last year [2008] I didn't understand the nuances of this requirement, so I just filled out our End of Year Assessment, and I included the link to my son's blog, thus effectively fulfilling the portfolio requirement. This year, I'll do the same, assuming that these meet the "superintendent's approval," unless told otherwise.

In grades 4–8, homeschooled NY [New York] students are required to file an annual assessment from the list of approved tests. . . . This is also to be administered by a person approved by the superintendent.

However, on alternate years, homeschooled students in grades 4–8 can submit a narrative instead of an assessment test. Thus, a homeschooled student can postpone taking a standardized test until fifth grade.

Taking Tests When You Don't Have To

As a third grader, Alex is not required to take an assessment test, but I'm a proactive kind of mom.

Generally, we don't do much testing at all. I can tell from looking at his work product, or discussing the subject, whether or not he understands the material. In recent months, we added weekly spelling tests, but that was as an incentive to memorize the words.

Since we're not required to file an assessment test, it's actually a good time to investigate our options, and take these tests without any worries.

In midyear, I printed out the NY state tests (for third grade) that all third graders in NY public schools took in 2008. Unlike the students in public schools who take the Language Arts Test in January, and the Mathematics Test in March, Alex took all the tests in one week. In the home setting, it just wasn't the stressful, big deal that it is in school.

We hadn't done any prep, as the test itself was a preparation, and there was nothing riding on the outcome. Not surprisingly, Alex did incredibly well on the language arts sections, but he missed questions on the math sections. I found

Testing Requirements for Virginia Homeschoolers

Testing option (i) of the homeschool law allows homeschoolers to choose *ANY* nationally normed standardized achievement test. Parents may choose from a variety of tests such as the Stanford Achievement Test, the Comprehensive Test of Basic Skills (CTBS), the California Achievement Tests (CAT), the Iowa Tests of Basic Skills (ITBS . . .), Science Research Associates (SRA), or the Woodcock-Johnson [Psycho-]Educational Battery.

For option (i) only the composite score for language arts and mathematics (the basic battery) must be submitted. The composite score includes all subtests for language arts and mathematics. Science and history test sections are not required. The student's composite score must be in the fourth stanine or higher (23rd percentile) in order to continue homeschooling.

Under option (ii), parents may submit an independent evaluation or present a portfolio to the division superintendent. If an independent evaluation or assessment is chosen, the evaluation letter must be completed by a person licensed to teach in any state, or a person with a master's degree or higher in an academic discipline who has knowledge of the child's academic progress.

Home Educators Association of Virginia,
"Testing and the Law—Frequently Asked Questions,"
September 3, 2008. www.heav.org.

out that he didn't have a strong grasp of time or money, but those were topics he hadn't gotten to in the third-grade Singapore Math [a math curriculum often used by homeschoolers] sequence. Again, not a big deal.

Last week, I pulled out the third-grade test-prep book that I ordered along with the CAT-E test [California Achievement Test-Elementary School, a commonly used standardized test], and gave it to Alex to work on independently. He delighted in an easy week, where he got to practice his bubble-filling skills.

This week, I administered both the PASS test [Personalized Achievement Summary System, a standardized test developed for homeschoolers] and the CAT-E test. A bit much, I know. This was not the highlight of our homeschool year, but now I have a good idea of what we'll use in the future.

We decided that we did not like the PASS test. We found some of the questions to be poorly written, and it was a lot longer than the CAT-E, 150 vs. 100 questions. Now, we know that when we are required to submit an assessment test, we'll choose the CAT-E. However, we won't bother with this again until we have to in fifth grade.

Reassuring and Helpful

It was reassuring to know that Alex was meeting state standards; actually, it's gratifying to know that Alex is performing well beyond these minimum standards. Even though he is doing exceedingly well, the tests also showed us that there were topics or skills that needed review and reinforcement.

For us, the tests are a safety net. Next year, I'll just have Alex take the free NY state tests at home, for our own edification.

As a homeschool educator, I'm able to use these tests in a way that never happens in the schools. I can see the results right away, and I can use that information to help Alex strengthen weak areas.

Just in case you're wondering if I've suddenly had a change of heart regarding NCLB [No Child Left Behind, a 2001 act of Congress that increased the use of testing in schools], let me be perfectly clear.

Although I'm using the same state tests that schools give to comply with the No Child Left Behind laws, I'm not a fan of mandatory testing in our public schools.

As it stands, these tests are for the benefit of the schools, not the students. And, I don't see the schools deriving much benefit, either.

In the public schools, teachers don't usually see the results until late in the school year, months after they administer the test. Although it is always possible that there is a teacher somewhere who looks at the individual student results and uses that information to help that student, that has *NOT* been my experience.

I've found that the information is not used in the current year, and it's unlikely to be used the next. My kids seemed to have teachers who preferred starting the year with a blank slate, with no undue influence from prior records. I don't know this for a fact, but my daughter's teachers didn't seem to know much about her at the beginning of the year.

State tests are an excellent assessment tool in the home-school, not so much in our public schools.

I like using the state tests as an assessment tool. It works for us, as it doesn't demand much of my son, and it comforts me to have empirical evidence that he is doing at least as well as his public school peers. If I were a more confident home-schooler, or one with years of teaching experience, I probably wouldn't bother with them at all.

For now, the test results are potent ammunition when I get those pesky questions from friends and strangers asking me how do I know that my homeschooled son is doing well academically. Well, the test results show that he is, at a minimum, "maintaining and doing as well as before."

> *"So, which do you want for your children? . . . The ability to give rote answers that conform to . . . the government's idea of what is vital to know . . . or . . . would you rather have them turn into true scholars?"*

Homeschoolers Should Not Take Standardized Tests

Terrie Lynn Bittner

Terrie Lynn Bittner is a freelance writer and the author of Homeschooling: Take a Deep Breath—You Can Do This! *In the following viewpoint, she argues that testing poorly measures student achievement. She adds that testing works even worse for homeschoolers, who tend to pursue a few subjects deeply rather than memorizing facts that, she says, can usually be looked up anyway. Testing, Bittner says, results in rote memorization rather than true learning. She concludes that testing is meant to hold schools accountable to parents. Since homeschoolers are taught by parents, the issue of accountability is irrelevant, and testing is unnecessary.*

Terrie Lynn Bittner, "Should Homeschoolers Be Forced to Take Standardized Tests?" Terriebittner.com, 2003–2010. www.terriebittner.com. Reproduced by permission.

As you read, consider the following questions:

1. What subjects does Bittner say are being eliminated because of testing?

2. According to Bittner, why are homeschoolers and public school students not competing on an equal basis in taking standardized tests?

3. According to Bittner, what do homeschoolers focus on learning how to do?

Many people feel that homeschoolers should be tested each year, as are public school students. They wonder how anyone will know if the children are learning. If a test is considered necessary for public school students, shouldn't all children have to endure them?

Testing Hurts Students

There are several problems with this theory. First of all, testing has not been proven to improve education in the public schools. In fact, many teachers complain that it is hurting education. In the desperate push to teach children the shallow skills measured by the tests, real learning is eliminated. Children in some areas are not even getting recess because there isn't time. Art, music, science . . . any subject not on a test is not taught. Any skill not on a test is considered unimportant. Unfortunately, thinking is not on the test . . . so thinking is often ignored in favor of rote memorization.

Testing does not adequately measure learning. Often tests are subjective or based on cultural standards. . . . I once saw a sample state test. The second-grade test required children to interpret a poem. This was not an essay. This was multiple-choice. I got the question wrong. (I received perfect scores on my literature interpretations in college.) If I couldn't get it right, how was a second grader supposed to read the mind of the tester? I wondered how there can be a wrong answer for

Comparison of ACT Test Scores of Public School and Homeschool Students, 2009

The ACT is a test used for college admission, similar to the SAT. ACT tests are scored on a scale from 1–36.

	Public School	Homeschool
Average score	21.1	22.5
Average percentile overall	50th percentile	88th percentile
Average language percentile	50th percentile	84th percentile
Average math percentile	50th percentile	84th percentile
Average social studies percentile	50th percentile	86th percentile
Average science percentile	50th percentile	86th percentile
Average reading percentile	50th percentile	89th percentile

TAKEN FROM: Tere Scott, "Homeschoolers Score Big on Standardized Tests Including ACT/SAT and Sign Up Begins For Local PSAT," Examiner.com, September 2, 2009. www.examiner.com.

an interpretation. Interpretation by definition is an opinion. In college, I was told by my professor that any answer I gave would be considered correct, as long as I could back it up. The multiple-choice test did not allow for explanation, differences of opinion, or differences in life experience.

Testing is affected by the mood of the child, his experience in test taking, his abilities and disabilities, and by his desire to do well. On any given day, a child could give a radically different performance than he might give on another day. While public school teachers see the tests in advance and their students are given practice tests, homeschoolers are not. They are hardly competing on an equal basis. In addition, taking a state-mandated test would require homeschoolers to teach a state-mandated curriculum, since the public school curriculum is designed to teach the test. The public schools are clearly failing at education, with far fewer than half their students reading and writing at grade level; does it make sense to require homeschoolers to mimic them?

Concepts, Not Facts

Testing cannot adequately measure the way homeschoolers learn. Homeschoolers often do not work systematically through a textbook. They usually prefer to dig deeply into a subject. They may read a very advanced book on the subject, rather than start at the beginning. The basics may get picked up along the way and some basics may get missed. Generally, they have a good grasp of the concepts, but frequently don't bother to memorize the details.

Is this a good idea? Try to remember all the facts you stuffed into your head when you were in school. Do you know them now? Most likely, you don't. Does it matter? Of course not. Facts can be easily looked up. It's the concepts that matter. Concepts take time to learn and cannot just be looked up in a book. Standardized tests don't measure concepts; they measure what is nearly always forgotten and can be looked up when needed. People easily memorize the facts they need in their daily lives; when the time comes, a well-trained student will be able to track down and learn the information. If they never need it, then time was not wasted that could have better been spent on more important learning.

Homeschooling generally focuses on learning how to learn. It is this that matters in the long run. When a public school student graduates, what has he learned? He may have thousands of facts temporarily filling his brain, but can he learn? If he wants to learn more about physics or history and can't afford to take a class, will he know how to study these subjects himself? Most traditionally schooled adults say, "Oh, I'd love to learn that, but I can't afford to go to school." Homeschoolers just go to the library and start reading. They know how to learn without a teacher. In general, homeschoolers should study each of the major subject areas, but it doesn't really matter what they learn. It is more important that they learn to love learning, and that they learn how to learn. With these skills, they are ready for a lifelong love affair with learning.

So, which do you want for your children? Dull facts, the ability to give rote answers that conform to some adult's idea of the correct answers, and the government's idea of what is vital to know (which might change tomorrow) or ... would you rather have them turn into true scholars?

Accountability

The final issue to consider is one of accountability. Why do schools have to give tests? It is not to be certain [that] individual children are learning. If a child does poorly on the test, it is likely that nothing will change in his education. The test is to measure the school, not the child. This is considered necessary because schools cost money and the people who pay it demand accountability. Parents pay for private schools, and they also usually demand test scores, to be sure they are getting what they paid for. Homeschools are not publicly funded, and therefore, should not need to account to the government.

The standards for homeschoolers who are tested are far higher than those for public school students. If a homeschooled child does badly on a standardized test, he can be forced into a public school and the homeschool can be closed. Imagine the consequences if this standard were applied to a public school. There would be no schools left standing if they were required to make all their students pass. Why should the government be allowed to demand a 100% success rate for homeschoolers when they cannot meet that standard themselves? Until they can show that they really know what should be taught and how, they should allow those with the courage and love to sacrifice for education [to] do so in peace.

> *"If parents choose not to utilize all of the amenities that a public school has to offer, that is their right, but it is unfair to require that they either use all of them or none at all."*

Homeschoolers Should Participate in Public School Athletics

Rebecca Wright

Rebecca Wright is a policy intern with the Tennessee Center for Policy Research. In the following viewpoint, she argues that homeschoolers should be allowed to participate in extracurricular school activities such as sports. Homeschoolers pay taxes, she argues, and just because they do not use all of a public school's resources does not mean they should be forbidden from using any. She adds that letting homeschool students participate in athletic events does not harm the school, while refusing them admission hurts those homeschoolers who want to play competitively or who hope to obtain sports scholarships to college.

Rebecca Wright, "Homeschool Students Belong in School Sports," *Jackson Sun*, July 26, 2009. Reproduced by permission of the author.

As you read, consider the following questions:

1. Who is Jason Taylor, and what does he have in common with Venus and Serena Williams?

2. What were the benefits the author received from Florida allowing access to public school amenities for homeschool students?

3. According to Wright, what organizations are against equal access for homeschooled students?

What do University of Florida football standout Tim Tebow, this year's [2007's] NFL Man of the Year Jason Taylor and tennis champions Venus and Serena Williams have in common? They are all homeschooled students who were able to participate in their local public schools' athletic programs.

Not in Tennessee

Unfortunately, homeschooled students in Tennessee don't have the opportunity to participate in public school–related athletics. State lawmakers recently punted on the issue, deferring a bill to provide homeschooled athletes equal access to public school athletics until next year.

Homeschooled students are allowed to participate in public school athletics in 24 states (it appears Tennessee is behind the curve). The outspoken support of former homeschoolers turned star athletes has generated public support for equal access legislation in four more states: Alabama, Louisiana, North Carolina and South Carolina.

Having been homeschooled myself for nine years in the state of Florida, which allows equal access to public school amenities for homeschooled students, I had the ability to participate in numerous public school extracurricular activities. This was very beneficial for me and many of my homeschooled peers. Participating in public school activities also gave me the

Tim Tebow, Homeschool, and Football

The [University of] Florida quarterback [Tim Tebow] was the youngest of Bob and Pam Tebow's five children, all of whom were homeschooled by their deeply religious parents. Because of a Florida law that allows homeschoolers to play sports in the public school district where they live, Tebow played football for Nease High School in Jacksonville.

There, he won a state title and national acclaim. A scholarship to Florida followed, and Tebow has since won a national championship and a Heisman Trophy.

Thing is, had Florida not enacted its law in 1996, Tebow wouldn't have played football in high school.

"None of them would have played," Tebow's father once told the *Florida Times-Union*. "We weren't going to back off our commitment to homeschooling just to go play football somewhere."

Jenni Carlson, "BCS National Championship: Tim Tebow a Shining Example for Homeschooled Athletes," NewsOK.com, January 2, 2009. http://newsok.com.

rare opportunity to intermingle with and learn from my public school peers, one of whom I married.

Currently the Tennessee Secondary School Athletic Association, Tennessee Education Association, Tennessee School Boards Association and the majority of the state's public schools are all against equal access for homeschooled students, but why? Participation in extracurricular activities isn't a right, they claim, and just because homeschooled families pay taxes doesn't give them a right to be involved in publicly funded athletic programs.

School Should Not Be All or Nothing

Homeschool families pay taxes to support public education and to have their students schooled at home. If parents choose not to utilize all of the amenities that a public school has to offer, that is their right, but it is unfair to require that they either use all of them or none at all. That would be like forbidding everyone who drives their own vehicle from using public buses ever again unless they agree to use public transportation exclusively. That's simply ridiculous.

I have found no evidence which shows that equal access has harmed the schools and school districts in the states that allow it. But there is an abundance of stories of homeschooled students in the state of Tennessee and elsewhere who claim that the state laws which forbid them from participating in public school athletics have been exceedingly detrimental to them.

Homeschooled athletes are getting gypped. A homeschooled athlete doesn't always have access to other athletic programs. And even if they do, what if they want to make a sport their career or their ticket to college? Are they really going to get the best exposure to scouts and the best chance to hone their skills by playing in small and/or noncompetitive leagues? A parent or student shouldn't have to choose between an opportunity to get a college scholarship and their right to be home educated.

With the number of homeschooling families on the rise, we as a state should not send the message that we (dare I use the word) discriminate against families whose only "fault" is that they exercised their right to choose their child's education.

| *"The camaraderie and friendships that are developing around these teams [are] amazing."*

Homeschoolers Should Organize Their Own Athletic Programs

Dari Mullins

Dari Mullins is a homeschool mother and a writer whose books include Galloping the Globe, *coauthored with Loreé Pettit. In the following viewpoint, she argues that homeschool sports teams offer opportunities that are not available through regular school teams. The homeschool leagues, she says, have greater camaraderie among players and give homeschool families a chance to bond that would not be available in a regular league setting.*

As you read, consider the following questions:

1. Where are the Trailblazers based?

2. Mullins was surprised that what group of players came to watch the middle school team?

3. According to Mullins, what do coaches of homeschool teams teach in addition to the sport?

Dari Mullins, "Why Play Homeschool Sports," HSinsider.com, Spring 2008. www .hsinsider.com. Reproduced by permission.

Picture this: A gym full of screaming fans cheering their team on—stands full of parents shouting for every point scored and athletes driven to keep going, even though they are losing and want to give up. Now the most shocking thing: This was a middle school basketball game and the stands included *HIGH SCHOOL* players who came to cheer their counterparts to a conference victory. Now, the team suffered [its] first conference loss (mind you, the starting point guard was sick), but a valuable lesson was learned and that is where *YOU* come in!!!

Friendship and Sportsmanship

The Trailblazers, a homeschool team based in Asheville, NC, are finishing up the winter season of their first year and are recruiting athletes to play spring sports, including baseball, softball and girls' soccer. There are many other homeschool sports organizations all over the nation. By searching homeschool sports on the Internet, you can access hundreds of Web sites of organizations that provide opportunities for homeschool athletes.

Now—back to the first paragraph. . . . The camaraderie and friendships that are developing around these teams [are] amazing. The game I mentioned above was played on Friday, January 11 [2008] at Emmanuel Lutheran School. The most astounding and exciting thing was not on the court, but in the stands. Many spectators had come to watch, but a group of 12 high school players came to watch the middle school team. Of the 12, only three had siblings playing in the game. How many high school athletes voluntarily go watch a middle school game? Seeing all of the energy and spirit that these kids are developing just compels me to share it with others. I know many homeschoolers play on rec [recreation] leagues, travel or other school teams (my children have also played for these other teams), but I would like to share with you some reasons to seriously consider playing with a homeschool team over any others.

Home-Schoolers and School Athletics

In the insular world of high school, where a few hundred kids spend six hours a day together and everyone knows everyone else's business, the transition from the classroom to the athletic field is virtually seamless. Same faces, different setting.

For the handful of home-schooled students who suit up for their local high schools, however, it's not always so easy. In some cases, earlier participation in youth sports programs like Little League means the faces are familiar regardless of the educational situation. . . .

Other times, though, the transition requires more finesse. For the Frisbie brothers, it meant playing as freshmen and potentially taking playing time away from their more experienced Kearsarge teammates. For Concord High's Mark Sullivan, also a freshman, it meant trying to fit in on the varsity team not just as an underclassman, but as a stranger to Concord [New Hampshire] and the school.

Donovan Burba,
"A Different Kind of Home Team,"
Concord Monitor, May 8, 2006.
www.concordmonitor.com.

Reasons for Homeschool Leagues

1. Lasting friendships with like-minded individuals—They play with other homeschoolers—they understand each other—no one teases, questions or ridicules them for being "different." They can talk freely about the struggles, frustrations, and triumphs of homeschooling because they understand each other.

2. Perseverance and competition—By playing at a middle school and [a] high school level, the students are pushed to achieve at a level not experienced before, which encourages them to achieve excellence in other areas of their lives. They learn to persevere through seemingly insurmountable obstacles.

3. Relationships with families who share the same values— Knowing the families of the friends my children have is invaluable. Since we all experience many of the same trials, fears, and concerns, I enjoy spending time with these parents. It also enables me to get to know them *BEFORE* my children are asking to spend time with their children.

4. Coaches who teach character as well as the sport—Most coaches for these teams realize the important role they play in the development of these students. They know that sports are not the [be-all] and end-all . . . but realize the lessons learned while playing will continue with them throughout their lives.

5. The privilege to be a role model for younger athletes— The younger students coming up are already talking about how they "can't wait to be a Trailblazer." This gives your student a chance to be a leader and a strong role model for these younger ones.

6. The opportunity to pursue athletics in college—Many sports have tournaments, which can provide recognition for your athlete. These tournaments are on state, regional and national levels. These tournaments can provide your student a chance to be seen by colleges or other higher level coaches.

Periodical Bibliography

The following articles have been selected to supplement the diverse views presented in this chapter.

Charlotte Gerber — "Homeschoolers and Public School Sports: Parents Sit on the Fence," FamilyLobby.com, 2008. http://articles.familylobby.com.

Heavenly Homemakers — "Homeschool Hubbub: What Curriculum?" July 21, 2009. http://heavenlyhomemakers.com.

Andrea Hermitt — "Is Testing Homeschoolers Really a Bad Idea?" Families.com Home Schooling Blog, August 22, 2009. http://homeschooling.families.com/blog.

Catherine Levison — "The Charlotte Mason Method in Brief," CharlotteMasonEducation.com. http://charlottemasoneducation.com.

Denise Oliveri — "Homeschool Testing Options: Finding the System That Works for Your Children," Suite101.com, May 3, 2007. http://homeschool-testing.suite101.com.

Susan Saulny — "Home Schoolers Content to Take Children's Lead," *New York Times*, November 26, 2006. www.nytimes.com.

Isabel Shaw — "Do Homeschoolers Miss Out on High School Sports and Activities?" FamilyEducation.com. http://school.familyeducation.com.

Successful Homeschooling Blog — "Public School Sports—Can Homeschoolers Have Their Cake and Eat It, Too?" January 5, 2009. http://successful-homeschooling.blogspot.com.

Jan Vroegin — "Evaluating Your Homeschooled Child's Progress," Helium. www.helium.com.

For Further Discussion

Chapter 1

1. In the middle of his viewpoint, Steve Shives includes an update, noting that contrary to his original assumption, most homeschoolers are not actually fundamentalist Christians. Does this undercut his argument about the dangers of homeschooling and the need to withhold diplomas from some homeschool students? Explain your reasoning.

2. The Minnesota Homeschoolers' Alliance (MHA) notes that one cannot determine whether homeschoolers are well socialized until "socialization" is defined. How does Margaret W. Boyce seem to define good socialization? How does her view of socialization differ from Michael F. Haverluck's view of socialization?

Chapter 2

1. Kimberly A. Yuracko argues that children have a constitutional right to a minimum level of education. Who does she feel may be guilty of violating that right? Who might Bruce N. Shortt accuse of violating that right? Who do you think has the better case, and what policy steps might be taken to guarantee children's right to a minimum level of education?

Chapter 3

1. Most of the viewpoints in this section focus on whether homeschooling will hurt or harm the children who are homeschooled. Name at least one exception in which the writer focuses on the effect of homeschooling not on homeschooled children, but on parents or society. Do you

think the writer you chose makes a convincing case, or do you think that the choice to homeschool should focus solely on the good of the child?

2. Pick either feminism or Christianity. How would you define the term you chose? Does your definition fit with the way the term is used by the writers in this chapter?

Chapter 4

1. Terrie Lynn Bittner says that "testing cannot adequately measure the way homeschoolers learn" and adds that "homeschools are not publicly funded, and therefore, should not need to account to the government." Do you think Sandra Foyt would agree with the first statement? The second statement? Both? Neither? Explain your answer.

Organizations to Contact

The editors have compiled the following list of organizations concerned with the issues debated in this book. The descriptions are derived from materials provided by the organizations. All have publications or information available for interested readers. The list was compiled on the date of publication of the present volume; the information provided here may change. Be aware that many organizations take several weeks or longer to respond to inquiries, so allow as much time as possible.

American Homeschool Association (AHA)
PO Box 759, Palmer, AK 99645-0759
(800) 236-3278
e-mail: Director@americanhomeschoolassociation.org
Web site: www.americanhomeschoolassociation.org

The American Homeschool Association (AHA) is a service organization created to network homeschoolers on a national level. It is sponsored in part by the publishers of *Home Education Magazine*. The AHA's Open Online Journalism project, or *AHA Citizen Journal*, provides news, information, and resources for homeschooling families.

California Homeschool Network (CHN)
2640 - A7 Myrtle Avenue, Monrovia, CA 91016
(800) 327-5339
e-mail: chn_mail@californiahomeschool.net
Web site: http://californiahomeschool.net

The California Homeschool Network (CHN) is an inclusive, all-volunteer organization dedicated to preserving educational freedom to homeschool. CHN monitors and responds to legislation that may threaten homeschoolers, educates homeschooling families and the public, and fosters community among homeschoolers. Its Web site includes information about homeschooling, resource links, guides to current California legislation, and a store from which to order CHN publications. It publishes the quarterly *CHN News*.

Center for Public Education
1680 Duke Street, Alexandria, VA   22314
(703) 838-6722 • fax: (703) 548-5613
e-mail: centerforpubliced@nsba.org
Web site: www.centerforpubliceducation.org

The Center for Public Education is a national resource for accurate, timely, and credible information about public education and its importance. An initiative of the National School Boards Association (NSBA), the center provides up-to-date research, data, and analysis on current education issues and explores ways to improve student achievement and engage public support for public schools. The center published the report *Defining a 21st Century Education* in July 2009.

Home School Legal Defense Association (HSLDA)
PO Box 3000, Purcellville, VA   20134-9000
(540) 338-5600 • fax: (540) 338-2733
e-mail: info@hslda.org
Web site: www.hslda.org

The Home School Legal Defense Association (HSLDA) is a national membership Christian organization of families who homeschool their children. Its goal is to defend and advance the constitutional right of all parents to direct the education of their children and to protect family freedoms. The organization supports homeschooling families by negotiating with local officials, serving as an advocate in court proceedings, monitoring federal legislation, and fighting any proposed laws perceived as harmful. Its Web site includes policy briefs, news items, and other resources.

Massachusetts Home Learning Association (MHLA)
164 Norfolk Street, Holliston, MA   01746

e-mail: netadmin1@mhla.org
Web site: www.mhla.org

The Massachusetts Home Learning Association (MHLA) is a voluntary unincorporated organization dedicated to advocacy for and education about homeschooling. It has no political or religious affiliation and aims to unify all homeschoolers in Massachusetts. Its Web site provides copies of legal documents relevant to homeschoolers, articles, resource links, and information about other statewide and national homeschool organizations. It publishes the *Guide to Homeschooling in Massachusetts*.

National Black Home Educators (NBHE)
13434 Plank Road, PMB 110, Baker, LA   70714
e-mail: contact@nbhe.net
Web site: www.nbhe.net

National Black Home Educators (NBHE) is a Christian online resource network founded in 2000 to encourage, support, and offer fellowship to all families interested in homeschooling. The organization provides information about starting homeschooling, connects veteran families with new families, and recommends resources such as books, music, films, speaking information, and curriculum. NBHE publishes a quarterly newsletter, *The Legacy*.

**National Challenged Homeschoolers Associated
Network (NATHHAN)**
PO Box 310, Moyie Springs, ID   83845
(208) 267-6246; (800) 266-9837
e-mail: nathanews@aol.com
Web site: www.nathhan.com

The National Challenged Homeschoolers Associated Network (NATHHAN) is a Christian organization dedicated to encourage and assist the homeschooling of special needs children. It maintains a discussion board, a directory, and a lending library for members. Its Web site also includes articles, links, and resources. NATHHAN/CHASK (Christian Homes and Special Kids) offers four brochures, including the *Adverse Prenatal Diagnosis* brochure and the *Straight Talk* brochure.

National Home Education Research Institute (NHERI)
PO Box 13939, Salem, OR   97309
(503) 364-1490 • fax: (503) 364-2827
e-mail: mail@nheri.org
Web site: www.nheri.org

The National Home Education Research Institute (NHERI) is a nonprofit research organization that collects, tracks, and analyzes research on home-based education. A clearinghouse of research for the public, researchers, homeschoolers, the media, and policy makers, the organization strives to educate the public about homeschooling research through speaking engagements, research reports, books, videos, and the journal *Home School Researcher*. Publications include the *Worldwide Guide to Homeschooling* and *Home Educated and Now Adults: Their Community and Civic Involvement, Views About Homeschooling, and Other Traits*.

SecularHomeschool.com
Web site: www.secularhomeschool.com

SecularHomeschool.com is a Web site devoted to providing resources and creating community among secular homeschoolers. The site includes blogs, forums, articles, and links to resources including local secular homeschooling groups.

U.S. Department of Education (ED)
400 Maryland Avenue SW, Washington, DC   20202
(800) 872-5327
e-mail: customerservice@inet.ed.gov
Web site: www.ed.gov

The U.S. Department of Education (ED) works to ensure equal access to education and to foster educational excellence. The department establishes policies on federal financial aid for education; provides grants to primary, secondary, and postsecondary education institutes; offers financial aid to students for postsecondary education; and underwrites education research. It produces hundreds of publications annually, including *Community Update*, which informs readers about available resources, services, and publications.

Bibliography of Books

Susan Wise Bauer and Jessie Wise — *The Well-Trained Mind: A Guide to Classical Education at Home.* 3rd ed. New York: W.W. Norton & Company, 2009.

Terrie Lynn Bittner — *Homeschooling: Take a Deep Breath—You Can Do This!* Denver, CO: Mapletree Publishing Company, 2004.

Bruce S. Cooper, ed. — *Homeschooling in Full View: A Reader.* Greenwich, CT: Information Age, 2005.

Elaine Cooper, ed. — *When Children Love to Learn: A Practical Application of Charlotte Mason's Philosophy for Today.* Wheaton, IL: Crossway Books, 2004.

Cathy Duffy — *100 Top Picks for Homeschool Curriculum: Choosing the Right Curriculum and Approach for Your Child's Learning Style.* Nashville, TN: Broadman & Holman Publishing Group, 2005.

Milton Gaither — *Homeschool: An American History.* New York: Palgrave Macmillan, 2008.

Rachel Gathercole — *The Well-Adjusted Child: The Social Benefits of Homeschooling.* Denver, CO: Mapletree Publishing Company, 2007.

John Taylor Gatto *Dumbing Us Down: The Hidden Curriculum of Compulsory Schooling.* Gabriola Island, BC, Canada: New Society Publishers, 2005.

David Guterson *Family Matters: Why Homeschooling Makes Sense.* New York: Harcourt Brace Jovanovich, 1992.

Bradley Heath *Millstones & Stumbling Blocks: Understanding Education in Post-Christian America.* Tucson, AZ: Fenestra Books, 2006.

Robert Kunzman *Write These Laws on Your Children: Inside the World of Conservative Christian Homeschooling.* Boston: Beacon Press Books, 2009.

Michael Leppert and Mary Leppert *The Homeschooling Book of Lists.* San Francisco: Jossey-Bass, 2008.

Grace Llewellyn *The Teenage Liberation Handbook: How to Quit School and Get a Real Life and Education.* 2nd ed. Eugene, OR: Lowry House Publishers, 1998.

Grace Llewellyn, ed. *Freedom Challenge: African American Homeschoolers.* Eugene, OR: Lowry House Publishers, 1996.

Susan A. McDowell *But What About Socialization?: Answering the Perpetual Home Schooling Question: A Review of the Literature.* Nashville, TN: Philodeus Press, 2004.

Susan A. McDowell and Brian D. Ray, eds.	*The Home Education Movement in Context, Practice, and Theory: A Special Double Issue of the Peabody Journal of Education.* Mahwah, NJ: Lawrence Erlbaum Associates, 2000.
Lisa Pyles	*Homeschooling the Child with Asperger Syndrome: Real Help for Parents Anywhere and on Any Budget.* London: Jessica Kingsley Publishers, 2004.
Brian D. Ray	*Worldwide Guide to Homeschooling: Facts and Stats on the Benefits of Homeschool.* Nashville, TN: Broadman & Holman Publishing Group, 2005.
Lisa Rivero	*The Homeschooling Option: How to Decide When It's Right for Your Family.* New York: Palgrave Macmillan, 2008.
Marilyn Rockett	*Home Schooling at the Speed of Life: Balancing Home, School, and Family in the Real World.* Nashville, TN: B & H Publishing Group, 2007.
Patricia Schetter and Kandis Lighthall	*Homeschooling the Child with Autism: Answers to the Top Questions Parents and Professionals Ask.* San Francisco: Jossey-Bass, 2009.
Mitchell L. Stevens	*Kingdom of Children: Culture and Controversy in the Homeschooling Movement.* Princeton, NJ: Princeton University Press, 2001.

Paul & Gena
Suarez, eds.

Homeschooling Methods:
Advice on Learning Style
TN: Broadman & Holm
Group, 2006.

Karen Taylor, ed.

The California Homescho
2nd ed. Hayward, CA: Ca
Homeschool Network/Vic
Canada: Trafford Publishi.

Douglas Wilson,
ed.

Repairing the Ruins: The Cla:
Christian Challenge to Modern
Education. Moscow, ID: Canon .
1996.

A

Abus
Aca
Ac
A

Textbooks
  creationist, 33–34
  vs. "living books"/experiences,
    143, 144, 154
Totals, homeschooled students, 16,
  48, 68, 75–76, 100
Transportation services, 27
Tutoring, 46, 99–100, 104, 105

U

Unions, teachers, 27, 100, 101
United Kingdom, 54–62
United Nations Committee on the
  Rights of the Child, 14
U.S. Department of Education
  creation, 121
  National Assessment of Edu-
    cational Progress (NAEP),
    86–87

V

Vahid, Frank, 20
Vineland Adaptive Behavior
  Scales, 39, 49

Violence in schools, 29, 48, 51–52,
  119, 122
Virginia testing requirements, 148
Volunteer opportunities, 46, 50,
  110

W

Walsh, Kate, 92
West, Natalie C., 14
Williams, Venus and Serena, 157
Wilson, Douglas, 122
Witnesses to Christ. *See* Evange-
  lism opportunities
Women's issues. *See* Feminist ho-
  meschooling; Incomes, mothers
Woodcock-Johnson Psycho-
  Educational Battery, 148
  See also Standardized tests
Worldliness. *See* Materialistic val-
  ues; Secular nature of public
  schools
Wright, Rebecca, 156–159

Y

Yuracko, Kimberly A., 74–83